FIGHTING FOR LIFE

Fighting

for

Life

Robert P. Casey

WORD PUBLISHING

DALLAS   LONDON   VANCOUVER   MELBOURNE

PUBLISHED BY WORD PUBLISHING

DALLAS, TEXAS.

Book design by Mark McGarry
Set in Electra

Casey Robert P. (Robert Patrick), 1932–
Fighting for life: the story of a courageous pro-life democrat whose own
brush with death made medical history / by Robert P. Casey.

P.   CM.

ISBN 0–8499–1224–5

1. Casey, Robert P. (Robert Patrick), 1932–

2. Governors—Pennsylvania—Biography.

3. Pro-life movement—Pennsylvania.

4. Pennsylvania—Politics and government—1951–   I. Title.

F155.3.C37A3   1996

974.8'04—dc20   96–12563

CIP

Printed in the United States of America
67890   RRD   54321

Ellen and I dedicate this volume to our grandchildren:

Jack McGrath
Ellen Casey McGrath
Daniel McGrath
Will McGrath

James Philbin
Sean Philbin
Marie Casey Philbin
Genevieve Philbin

Nora Brier
Patrick Brier
Bobby Brier
Aileen Brier

Elyse Casey
Caroline Casey
Julia Casey

Ellen Walsh
Leo Walsh
Matthew Walsh
Rosemary Walsh

Amy Elizabeth Casey

to the children of Pat and Anne
and Bobby and Terese, expected in the fall,
and to those grandchildren who
may come along later.

Contents

Acknowledgments

ONE OF THE THEMES of this book is the sheer luck that seems to have followed me through sixty-four years of life. It was certainly with me in the writing of my story. I have been blessed with the help of many talented and dedicated people who guided me at every turn. A full accounting of my debts to those people would run page after page. But I must at least mention those whose contributions were most vital.

The work began with my meetings with Lynda Rutledge Stephenson. In our long and enjoyable conversations, Lynda helped me focus my ideas for the book. Without her help organizing the raw material—especially the material concerning my medical odyssey—I don't know how I would ever have begun writing my story.

I could never have made it through this project without my executive assistant, Bonnie Seaman. It's hard to think of any work I have done these past ten years without Bonnie. Another theme of this book is loyalty, and few people have taught me more about the trait than Bonnie.

I am deeply indebted to her for the skill and good spirit she brings to our work right up to this day.

Throughout the book I have tried to do justice to the unfailing encouragement and sound advice I have always received from my wife, Ellen, and our children—an impossible task. Here, special mention must go to my son, Chris. It was Chris who, when I began losing direction, came up with the idea of alternating chapters between past and present, from the story of my life to the story of my encounter with death. That idea transformed my book from a chronological narrative to what I hope is a richer and more engaging story.

Chris's suggestion, however, meant going back to page one and starting anew. Not an easy task. It was then that I called on Matthew Scully, a journalist who also worked with me as a speechwriter in my final years as governor. Ever since January 1992, when a *Washington Post* op-ed article by Matthew caught my eye, we have made a great team, and I have come to value his friendship as much as his way with words.

From there, I nervously handed the manuscript on to a team of demanding editors—all named Casey. Editorial comments ranged from "Not bad" to "Needs work" to "You're not going to tell *that* story again, are you?" At first I resisted the "chilling effect" of these edits. In fear, however, that they may one day write books of their own, I heeded their advice, and some of the funnier stories of our family life will just have to be handed down by oral tradition.

Of course, their advice and editing was, as always, sensible and thorough, and the book is far better for it. Ellen did double-duty as my inspiration and copy editor. In one way she made the writing more difficult: by bringing more joy into my life than I could ever convey with pen and paper.

I am grateful to Jeffrey Bell, Robert George, John DiIulio, and Frank Cannon for reading the manuscript and giving me the benefit of their helpful insights and recommendations. Each of them, together with John Mueller, John Wauck and Matthew Scully, was a player in the story of my presidential exploratory committee recounted in the final chapter of the book.

Finally, I thank the people of Pennsylvania and America who put their trust in me and, when I was down, lifted me up with their prayers. The story that follows will reflect, I hope, an equal faith in them and a belief that no problem or affliction is so great that we cannot overcome it together.

Robert P. Casey
Scranton, Pennsylvania
April 1996

1

A Milestone

There was nothing dramatic about it. Just a deep silence inside, and in that silence a voice saying, "Fight!"

OFTEN THE GREATEST TESTS in life are those we do not even notice until they are upon us. There is no chance of escape, appeal, or relief. One moment we're going along our way; the next moment we're surrounded on every side by trouble. No time to prepare. No transition. No warning, no bargaining, no debating, no equivocation. The problem just surrounds us and begins closing in. All the things and titles and powers we have gathered up in life fall away. What remains is the raw desire to survive. At such moments we meet ourselves for the first time.

For me, such a test came in November 1990. At the time I was riding high. I had just won re-election as governor of Pennsylvania. I had not only won, but prevailed by the biggest margin in the state's history. I had the political power that comes with such a vote of confidence. The wind was at my back. It was a milestone in my life, promising new opportunities and justifying past struggles. I was happy, relieved, fulfilled, proud.

It all began—as such ordeals so often do—with a routine visit to the doctor after the election. I had no particular symptoms, just wanted a clean bill of health before starting my second term. The only change I remember was that during periods of exercise, I found myself unable to walk as fast as usual. I also remember feeling a bit weary, more than the usual fatigue that comes with the final election frenzy.

At Hershey Medical Center, I was put through a long series of tests. The center is not far from Harrisburg, the state capitol. The doctors there had been looking after me since my heart bypass surgery several years before.

Things were going fine. Nothing unusual. But then came the last test, an examination of the muscles of the heart. My cardiologist, Dr. David Leaman, took one look at the results and said: "There seems to be a difference between the results of the test we just took and the same test that we took about eighteen months ago. I'm not sure whether this is a little problem or a big problem. But I think it best that we have a biopsy of the heart to make sure that we know exactly what we're dealing with here."

A biopsy was arranged. The word is now so familiar that those who haven't gone through a biopsy cannot know what a thoroughly unpleasant, invasive procedure it is. The doctors put a wire through a vein in my leg. Guiding the wire up to my heart, they then used a claw on the end of the wire to take a bit of tissue from the heart.

I had an uneasy feeling about it all. But anyone would feel a little apprehensive waiting to hear test results, especially after he's just felt a tiny claw making its way to his heart. I shook the fears off. I just wanted the whole business over with. After many hard-fought political battles, I was finally on top. I had things to do. I felt, I suppose, a little resentful at this whole intrusion into my life just when things were looking so good.

Time passed, and gradually the problem receded from my mind. It was probably nothing. Everything would be okay. I'd already been through a quadruple bypass operation: That had been my test, my allotted share of tribulation, and I'd passed it.

Only when the day came to hear the results from Dr. Leaman did I begin to focus again on the tests and what it all might mean. That night my wife, Ellen, and I finished dinner and went upstairs to the second floor library of the governor's residence. Dr. Leaman was to call at 7:00 P.M. The phone in the library had a speaker function, and I wanted to hear the news with Ellen at my side. We waited a few minutes and, right on schedule, the phone rang.

"Hello, Doctor. Well, how does it look?"

"To be honest, Governor, not very good. It's amyloid."

I didn't hear anything else for a few seconds. The only times I'd ever heard that word were in connection with the deaths of two Pennsylvania mayors I'd known well. They both died of a rare disease called amyloidosis, for which there was no cure and no treatment of any kind. It didn't take much for my mind to stretch "amyloid" into "amyloidosis."

The only time I'd ever felt so completely numb was a decade earlier, when I was told Ellen had a malignancy which could kill her. That news had been like a sledgehammer delivered to the head. And now I was being told I had a rare disease that would surely kill me.

We went back to our room and, after a silence, I explained to Ellen the amyloidosis cases of Richard Caliguiri, mayor of Pittsburgh, and Louis Tullio, mayor of Erie. Recalling their deaths, the situation really began to sink in. I was in trouble.

I can't say why, but when the shock passed I did not have any feeling of devastation or despair. There would be low points, but that night as I went to sleep, turning it all over in my mind, a strange feeling of hope came over me. I knew I was facing something big, something as serious as I'd ever faced. And yet I absorbed Dr. Leaman's words with a feeling of acceptance and defiance all at once. There was nothing dramatic about it. Just a deep silence inside, and in that silence a voice saying, "Fight!"

A few days later Ellen and I sat and talked about this new word, "amyloid," with my doctors. They did their best, but all they could offer was explanation—nothing in the way of encouragement. Very few doctors, they said, even encounter "amyloid" in a lifetime of practice. It can systematically destroy major organs of the body. Death from the disease can come quickly or slowly. All they could tell us that night was that in the entire country—in fact, the entire world—only a few specialists knew more than that. As one of the doctors put it, "There are fewer doctors who know about amyloid than there are governors." They recommended that I consult with one of these specialists—Dr. Robert Kyle of the Mayo Clinic in Rochester, Minnesota.

That evening Ellen and I discussed whether or not we should tell our eight children. Christmas was coming, and after that our second inauguration. Why spoil Christmas for the kids with bad news that might, after all, be premature? We didn't have all the facts yet. Maybe Dr. Kyle would find something which would give me some hope. At the very least, we agreed that we should wait for a final diagnosis before telling our children.

We contacted Dr. Kyle and he came to the governor's residence in Harrisburg to examine me. While trying to be as encouraging as possible, he was also very clinical and precise, never hedging on the hard truth that mine was a disease with no cure and no treatment. Up to this point, the doctors were fairly certain I had "primary amyloidosis," the form of the disease which is most serious and deadly. After looking at the blood tests I'd undergone for him, he urged further tests before making a final diagnosis. We didn't know it at the time, but it would be almost six months before Dr. Kyle would make that final diagnosis.

The days and weeks and months moved along. Christmas came and went. Ellen and I kept to our resolve not to tell our children and their families. It was difficult to know such a thing and not share it. Between the time I heard, "It's amyloid," that night in November and the following summer, I passed through the most difficult and lonely period in my life. It was a time I could never have endured without Ellen.

The mood on Inauguration Day in January 1991 was anything but joyful, for bigger reasons than my own troubles. As a family, we had just lost our beautiful niece, Judy Murray—a thirty-five-year-old mother of three—to breast cancer. We would be burying her the next day. Around America, people were still suffering from the worst recession in over fifty years, a recession deeply felt in Pennsylvania. The Gulf War had begun and American ground and air forces were to enter the war that night.

The air was filled with speculation about the possibility of heavy American losses in the ground fighting. There was a pall over the crowd, a sense of foreboding. To make things even more tense, the State Police warned us to expect a demonstration during the ceremony by Act-Up, a group of radical AIDS activists.

As the inaugural procession filed onto the platform for the ceremony, the demonstrators' yelling, screaming, and cursing began. Several dozen of them were at the front of the crowd. The noise was deafening, their message laced with insults and obscenities, directed at me. Some of the demonstrators carried coffins through the crowd together with cardboard tombstones that read, "Bob Casey, R.I.P."

I had to remind myself that these angry demonstrators saw me that day more as a symbol than as a fellow human being with problems of his own. I knew I'd done what I could to meet the AIDS epidemic.

I had made huge increases in the AIDS appropriation in Pennsylvania's budget. We'd set up a special state office to deal with AIDS. We'd even set aside state money for new AIDS drugs authorized by the Food and Drug Administration, making sure experimental drugs would be available even if federal money didn't provide them. Later, we would help Mother Teresa's order of nuns establish a hospice to care for terminally ill AIDS patients in Chester, Pennsylvania. Through our program of healthcare for the poor, we would also become prime supporters of another hospice for AIDS patients — Betak House in Philadelphia.

But on Inauguration Day, none of this seemed to matter much. When I rose to speak, the shouting only grew louder. I tried to ignore it, to talk over them. Then I tried confronting them: "There is hardly a family in Pennsylvania," I said above the din, "which doesn't know the meaning of suffering, of having to deal with an incurable disease."

More shouting, more insults, more obscenities. It was like talking to the wind. I still remember that moment as among the most deeply discouraging of my life.

2

Inscrutable Darkness

It was a journey that held a threat of endlessness.

IT'S HARD for me to explain what that moment meant to me, being sworn in a second time as the forty-second governor of Pennsylvania. For some years I'd been known to some opponents in the state's political circles as "The Three-Time Loss from Holy Cross." It was a nickname given me by a rival in my fourth run for governor. I wore the sobriquet with a certain pride. After defeating that opponent the fourth time around, I gladly gave it up.

But there's still something I like in the name. It captures something about my life and my whole idea of America itself.

As a boy, my father had worked in the coal mines. Orphaned as a teenager, he had supported his brothers and sisters. Yet somehow he managed to work himself through law school, joining the Pennsylvania bar at age forty. That's America. We're the country not only of the second chance—but the third and fourth. In America, anyone willing to fail, pick himself up, and try again still has a shot. No one is ever counted out. The story of America is the story of countless improbable comebacks, of persistent nobodies rising in the world, and in success never forgetting others still struggling.

It doesn't always work that way, but that's the idea; that's what makes us a great nation, our belief that no one's fate is set in stone.

Seeing that on paper, it seems to sit there like a cliché. I can only say that for me it has been a living faith. My father's whole life bore witness to it, much more than my own. I have tried to pass the same faith on to my children, so they will never forget the labor and sacrifice done in their name long before they were ever born.

When I think of my father, I think of his hands. The nails on all ten fingers had been ruined, broken and split permanently, as if someone had taken a knife and carved a ridge right through most of them. The end of his right middle finger was smashed so badly that it was splayed flat as though a boxcar had landed on it. Those hands were the very image of the forces that shaped his life, and the attitude toward life he instilled in me.

His name was Alphonsus Liguori Casey. He was named after Saint Alphonsus Liguori, an Italian saint of the Catholic Church who founded the Redemptorist order of priests. I believe the name was suggested by a nun at Saint Rose School in Carbondale, Pennsylvania. The co-founder of her order, the Immaculate Heart of Mary, was a Redemptorist priest, and the order's early beginnings were aligned with the famous Alphonsus.

My father's name was one you don't hear very much. Growing up his friends and family called him "Al" — or sometimes "Phonsie." But I was always proud of the name, "Alphonsus." One after another I encouraged my sons to adopt it as a confirmation name. Finally, after several failed attempts, our youngest son, Matt, took the name as his own. Matthew Alphonsus Casey. A strong name. A proud name. A name with character.

Around the turn of the century, when my father was eleven years old, he went to work in the anthracite coal mines around Carbondale, in the northeastern part of Pennsylvania. At that time, coal was king. Under the ground lay heavy deposits of anthracite coal, the richest deposits in the world.

Most of the members of my father's family—his father, uncles, and cousins—worked in and around the coal mines. Child labor, of course, was fairly common in those days. Some boys worked as "door tenders," opening the doors for the coal-laden cars straight from underground. Some worked with the mules that pulled the coal cars. And some worked in the "breaker," a large building with a conveyor belt in which the coal was broken up into different sizes. The "breaker boys" would straddle the conveyor belt and pick the rock, slate, and other debris from the belt as it moved by them. The children would do this work without gloves, just their small, bare-skinned hands.

Such hands were one of the hallmarks of a coal-mine worker. Then there were the permanent marks of injuries, the blue spider marks that remained long after the cuts and bruises had healed. The methods of cleaning the wounds were so primitive, particularly around the work site, that men of all ages were left with bluish marks on their heads, faces, hands, arms, anywhere the flesh had been broken and the dirt had not been completely removed from the wound. The marks often formed spider-like patterns beneath the skin.

Eleven-year-old Alphonsus worked with the mules. The job consisted of walking beside the mule from the depths of the coal mine to the surface, as the animal pulled the loaded coal car. Leather reins connected the mule to the car. Boys would guide the mules, grabbing up the reins when they'd fall to the ground, then replacing them. Boys also would help couple and uncouple the cars, and their hands would get caught between moving metal parts. A mule would only have to pull forward suddenly for the two metal surfaces to close on boys' fingers. The possibilities for injuries were unlimited, and that was just for the children.

For all the coal miners, danger was everywhere—from methane gas explosions to collapsing roofs. When the men stopped for lunch, they would sit on the ground, open their lunchpails, and eat their sandwiches. They seldom finished their sandwiches though. They would always leave a bit of bread—a blackened piece, the part that they had been holding with coal-dirty hands, discarding it into a corner of the work area as they finished.

Picture an eleven-year-old boy seeing the blackened bread tossed into a corner, and then in a few moments, watching the rats run up, snatching the bread and scurrying away. For the men and boys, the rats were welcome signs: As long as there were rats living down there, it meant no deadly gas there either.

The novelist Stephen Crane toured a mine near Scranton in 1894, just ten years before my father went to work in the mines. He described the scene in *McClure's* Magazine:

> The breakers squatted upon the hillsides and in the valley like enormous preying monsters, eating of the sunshine, the grass, the green leaves. The smoke from their nostrils had ravaged the air of coolness and fragrance. All that remained of vegetation looked dark, miserable, half-strangled. . . .
>
> The [boys] . . . are not yet at the spanking period. One continually wonders about their mothers, and if there are any schoolhouses. But as for them, they are not concerned. When they get time off, they go out on the culm heap and play baseball. . . . And before them always is the hope of one day getting to be door-boys down in the mines; and, later, mule boys; and yet later, laborers and helpers. . . .

A guide then led Crane into the mine:

> It was a journey that held a threat of endlessness. Then suddenly the dropping platform slackened its speed. It began to descend slowly and with caution. At last, with a crash and a jar, it stopped. Before us stretched an inscrutable darkness, a soundless place of tangible loneliness. Into the nostrils came a subtly strong odor of powder-smoke, oil, wet earth. The alarmed lungs began to lengthen their respirations.
>
> Our guide strode abruptly into the gloom. His lamp flared shades of yellow and orange upon the walls of a tunnel that led away from the foot of the shaft. Little points of coal caught the light and shone like diamonds. . . .
>
> The wonder of these avenues is the noise — the crash and clatter of machinery as the elevator speeds upward with the loaded cars and drops thunderingly with the empty ones. The place resounds with the shouts of mule boys, and there can always be heard the noise of approaching coal cars, beginning in mild rumbles and then swelling down upon one in a tempest of sound. In the air is the slow painful throb of the pumps working at the water which collects in the depths. There is booming and banging

and crashing, until one wonders why the tremendous walls are not wrenched by the force of this uproar. And up and down the tunnel there is a riot of lights, little orange points flickering and flashing. Miners stride in swift and somber procession. But the meaning of it all is in the deep bass rattle of a blast in some hidden part of the mine. It is war. It is the most savage part of all in the endless battle between man and nature. Sometimes their enemy becomes exasperated and snuffs out ten, twenty, thirty lives. Usually she remains calm, and takes one at a time with method and precision. She need not hurry. She possesses eternity. After a blast, the smoke, faintly luminous and silvery, floats silently through the adjacent tunnels. . . .

Great and mystically dreadful is the earth from the mine's depth. Man is in the implacable grasp of nature. It has only to tighten slightly, and he is crushed like a bug. His loudest shriek of agony would be as impotent as his final moan to bring help from that fair land that lies, like Heaven, over his head. There is an insidious, silent enemy in the gas. If the huge fanwheel on the top of the earth should stop for a brief period, there is certain death. If a man escapes the gas, the floods, the squeezes of falling rock, the cars shooting through little tunnels, the precarious elevators, the hundred perils, there usually comes to him an attack of miner's asthma that slowly racks and shakes him into the grave. Meanwhile, he gets $3 per day, and his laborer $1.25.

In this world my father lived out his youth. In the year of Crane's visit, there were 140,000 hard-coal miners working in Pennsylvania and 86,000 soft-coal miners. In that year, 446 of the former were killed, and 123 of the latter. The worst year was 1907: a total of 1,516 were killed in the mines. From 1870 to 1968, there some 31,047 known fatalities in the anthracite mines of Pennsylvania.

Alphonsus's nearest brush with danger was caused by what the men called "kicking the traces." The leather straps or reins on the back of the mules were called "traces." The mules would shrug and kick the traces off their backs. My father's boyhood job was to pick up the straps and replace them on the mule's back. "Kicking the traces" meant bucking, throwing off restraints, going one's own way.

In a way it would become a metaphor for my dad's own life. But during his early years it meant just one thing, getting those leather straps back around whichever ornery mule he was responsible for. Doing this one day, Alphonsus bent down to pick up one of those leather straps and when he did, the rear hooves of the mule kicked him square in the face.

The expression, "kick like a mule," has always held for me the image of those scars on my father's face, scars he bore until his death. A mule kick can kill a man, and it should have killed my father there and then. How an eleven-year-old boy survived a kick square in the face, I don't know—but somehow he did. My father said that kick hurled him over a loaded five-foot-high coal car and into the wall of the mine—the "face" of the mine, as miners would say. His nose was smashed and he had an open wound from his forehead across his eyebrow, down his nose, through his lip, and into his chin.

No ambulance was called. No paramedics came to save him. Work didn't even stop. That was how things were done at the turn of the century. He picked himself up and staggered for help. The people in charge of the mine wrapped a bandage around his head, then turned him over to another boy his age who was ordered to take him home to his mother. Unable to see much through the bloody bandage, he let the boy guide him slowly home—but perhaps not slowly enough.

The most vivid memory my father had of that long walk home was of a foot bridge. Somehow in trying to cross it, both boys lost their footing and fell into the dirty coal slurry below. The slurry carried the black water from the coal washing operation off the mine's property, so when they fished themselves out of the water, the bandage around my father's head was black and wet with slurry.

Once he finally made it home, his mother called a doctor and they laid him down on the dining room table, where the doctor sewed the long gouge in his face back together. There were no benefits—no worker's compensation, no safety net in place to take care of the adult worker, much less an injured child.

After I was elected governor in 1986, the Historical and Museum Commission did some research on my ancestors. They found census records from the year 1900 for Carbondale, Pennsylvania. It was an authentic record of the generations before my father's—my great-grandparents and all their children including my paternal grandfather, whose name was Thomas. It appears from the records that my great-great-grandparents were the ones who made the trip to America from Ireland.

My great-grandfather, Edward, came as a one-year-old child in 1851, which was the time of the Great Hunger, as Irishmen refer to it. The Irish potato famine began in 1845 and forced the vast migration of the Irish across the globe. And many of those who came to northeastern Pennsylvania had gone immediately to work in the mines.

My grandfather's brothers, Michael (age twenty-six), Martin (twenty-four), William (nineteen), and Joseph (fourteen) all worked in the mines in 1900. My grandfather would become a fireman, a man who shoveled the coal into the furnaces that provided all the energy for the mines. He would die young, in his thirties.

The census also listed the other people on the block where my great-grandparents raised my grandfather, Thomas. They were Hungarians and they, too, came here to work in the coal mines.

And under Thomas's name were listed the children of Thomas and my paternal grandmother, Sarah, whose maiden name was Haggerty. There was Alphonsus and his older brother, Edward, younger brother, Benedict, and sisters, Margaret and Leonora. I can recall my dad telling me about his younger sister, whom he called Nora, who died in the influenza epidemic in 1917. Thomas and Mary were children of Thomas and Sarah, born after 1900 and thus not listed on the census.

My father often talked about what it was like as a child to listen to the miners and see them persevere in a job that was miserable and dark and life-threatening, beginning to end. Not that the men complained of these afflictions. On the contrary; even as they hoped for better things, most were proud of the work and the skill they brought to it. My dad admired their tenacity, their toughness and courage. And he often talked about how skilled the miners were. They had to know how to handle dynamite and perform a wide range of tasks requiring great skill and judgment learned over many years. What he saw gave him an abiding respect for working people, a respect that would drive him toward a law degree late in life and a professional career dedicated to helping working people.

Even as my father opened new professional paths for me, he left me with a respect for working people and their struggles. I could go far in life but if I lost that, I would be nothing.

In the courtyard which adjoins the main entrance to the governor's residence in Harrisburg stands a bronze sculpture depicting a massive figure putting in place a large piece of steel. The sculpture is entitled "The Pennsylvania Worker." I had it placed there so that all future occupants of that residence, and the people of Pennsylvania whom they represent, would never forget the sweat and blood of working men and women who built Pennsylvania, forged the Industrial Revolution in our country, and outproduced the world. When I look at that sculpture, I see my father's hands.

3

Somebody Out There

*With campaign-like intensity, I began to canvass the doctors
and contacts I'd been writing and calling since my diagnosis.
I still refused to accept the verdict that nothing could be done
to cure my condition.*

THERE'S ONE great advantage to losing: It teaches you to understand the value of what you're seeking.

During my eight years as governor, I felt every day was a remarkable opportunity. I'm always a little wary of politicians who talk about the burdens and trials of public office, as if it were all thrust upon them against their will. I say, "If it seems a burden rather than a privilege, you're in the wrong business." Public office never for one moment seemed a burden to me. I was thrilled and honored to be there. I'd spent enough time in pursuit of the governor's office and wasn't about to start complaining of its difficulties. My idea of a burden was going into a coal mine before dawn five or six days a week. Waking up each morning in a governor's residence—with opportunities my father never had, opportunities he himself gave me—that was no burden.

If I ever did come close to weariness, though, it was during those first few months of 1991. I had just been told I was slowly dying. On top of that, in those same winter months, I underwent the fight of my political life.

In part, it was a fight against my own instincts. In the middle of a bitter recession, I had to cut $700 million from Pennsylvania's budget, shutting down government institutions and laying off thousands of government workers. I had no choice, but that didn't make it any easier. The recession had knocked the bottom out of the state's revenues. I had to raise taxes, too, or else see the state fall into even deeper financial trouble.

Neither move did much for my public image. Hailed in November and re-elected by a resounding million votes, in some quarters I was now branded a "liar" and worse. The defeated Republican gubernatorial challenger, Barbara Hafer, accused me of deliberately hiding the state's fiscal problems during the campaign.

But my conscience was clear. My campaign statements reflected the economic facts as I knew them. The election was in November. Even Alan Greenspan, chairman of the Federal Reserve, didn't call it a recession until the following January. I had been careful to state publicly that, because the economy was so volatile, I could not repeat the "no tax-increase" pledge I'd made and kept during my first term. But all this did not make the charges and criticism any easier to endure. They hurt.

It wasn't as if I enjoyed throwing people out of work or raising taxes. In fact there would have been no more certain road to popularity than to delay this course of action and live on borrowed time until the inevitable collapse, by which time maybe somebody else would be governor and charged with cleaning up the mess. Having to put people out of work was sickening. It sure was not what I'd come this far to do. I had pledged to help people, to create jobs for them and protect the jobs they had. So many once-flourishing steel and coal towns were blighted by unemployment and all the ills that came with it.

One of my campaign promises during the 1986 gubernatorial campaign was to fly to one of these towns, Monessen, on the very first day of my first term as governor to start doing something about economic development. And on the first day, I had done just that. Soon, job programs and training centers were up and running, economic development loans were being funded, and high-tech companies were setting up shop around the state. Little by little, healing came to the gaping wound that steel and coal had left when the world turned away from those century-long kings of Pennsylvania production. We were beginning to turn things around. But then the recession came. And now it was necessary to lay people off and raise taxes. As I saw it, there was no getting around that necessity.

When the budget fight in our politically divided state legislature began, the controversy and contention were worse than I'd ever seen. I felt up to the battle, and yet in a way removed from it, impatient with all the haggling and maneuvering and accusations. This time around, I quite literally did not have time for it. I'd done my share of haggling and maneuvering over the years—don't get me wrong. Day-to-day politics never has been and never will be a pretty business. But I did at times feel a bit removed from things, isolated by problems that could not be argued, compromised, or vetoed away.

Rumors about my health had begun making the rounds. My staff reported hearing them everywhere. In general the rumors were inaccurate—one paper had me suffering from cancer—but rumors always have a life of their own. For all practical purposes, I was still functioning quite well. There was trouble ahead, but exactly what lay in store for me was still unclear. Why make any public statements before a final diagnosis?

It arrived in April 1991. Dr. Kyle pronounced that instead of primary amyloidosis, the most aggressive form, mine was a form only recently discovered—"Appalachian familial amyloidosis."

This disease was found in a very small number of people in the United States. Almost all of the people diagnosed with it were members of the same families. These families had been found in Kentucky and West Virginia, the Appalachian region of the United States, with one diagnosed family living in Chicago. And all had ancestors who came from Ireland.

The upshot was that I still had amyloidosis, and it was still progressive, but this kind had a longer fuse. That is, people with the disease could live longer than those with primary amyloidosis. The disease was still fatal—no cure and no treatment. But at least I had time. How much time, I didn't know. Since so few cases were documented of this strain, no one knew when the clock would begin to run in any single case. So there was still a chance. Anything could happen.

With that, it was time to clear the air and tell the people of Pennsylvania about my disease. First, though, we had to tell the kids.

"Dad would like everyone to come to Scranton for Mother's Day," Ellen told our children. She had wanted to tell them more, and they wanted her to, but she had held back. They all began to talk among themselves, of course, of our strange behavior, of this unusual request.

We rarely asked the whole group to be anywhere at one time. In the first place, logistically, it was almost impossible—we had eight children, most of them well into creating families of their own. Four lived in Pennsylvania, two in Connecticut, one in Washington, D. C., and the youngest attended college in Indiana. But also, we just weren't the type of parents who ever made such "command performances," as one of our daughters put it. This time, though, I wanted everyone to be there to hear it all firsthand, including the spouses. There had been enough rumors. And I would stress the importance of keeping it all to ourselves until I had time to hold a press conference.

On Mother's Day weekend, with everyone crowded into our living room in Scranton, I told the children what I knew. "I have been diagnosed with a disease called Appalachian familial amyloidosis," I said. "While there is no known cure or treatment, the doctors say that the disease has a relatively long course. Matters could be a lot worse. I could have primary amyloidosis, which is immediately life-threatening."

Then I told the children the part that would most affect them. "The disease is thought by the doctors to be hereditary. So that means there's a fifty/fifty chance some of you will be affected. To find out, all you have to do is take a simple blood test." Then I added, "But it looks like though, the strain of amyloid I have has a relatively late onset compared to some strains. My symptoms didn't begin, as far as we can tell, until I turned fifty-six."

Then I dialed Dr. Kyle, who had graciously made himself available, and placed him on the speakerphone for all to hear. He explained all that medical science knew about the nature of the disease. It was quiet in the room for a moment; then the questions began.

My children learned how the genetic condition could kill, protein invading major organs, shutting things down. They now knew the odds were that some of them might go through this ordeal someday too. But not one question had to do with their own chances of having amyloidosis. Not one of them seemed to hear the part about their own potential genetic problems. Their only questions were about what amyloidosis meant for me.

Several weeks later, in June 1991, I called a press conference in Harrisburg and read my statement. Dr. Leaman and Dr. Graham Jeffries, an internist at Hershey Medical Center, were there, and Dr. Kyle spoke to the press by speakerphone from Little Rock, Arkansas. The reporters questioned me and the doctors down to the last detail. Every conceivable question about this obscure condition must have been asked. The resulting news reports were no longer based on rumor, but were finally accurate. Thankfully, after media stories about my health seemed to be everywhere I looked, curiosity about "the governor's health issue" subsided for the time being. Now everyone knew.

I moved on immediately to the inevitable challenges—that year they came as never before. Looking back, the rush of events seems a blessing. Given time enough, I'd have sat back and thought about my troubles as much as the next person—maybe more, because mine would be a drawn-out death. Luckily, I didn't have time to sit around thinking about myself. "He who has a *Why* can bear almost any *How*," someone has said. I was lucky enough to have a *Why*, a reason to go on, a reason to fight. Next to my wife and family, work was my best ally.

In this way, 1991 and 1992 came and went. I did more, not less, and found work to be the best therapy. Soon, though, I could feel trouble approaching. Work was going along without a hitch, but I began to notice weakness in my legs, and nausea. These were bad signs, and no work or cause could distract me from them. If there was going to be any way out of this, I had to find it—and find it now.

I had been in contact with the few amyloidosis experts in the country besides Mayo's Dr. Kyle, namely Dr. Merrill Benson in Indianapolis, and Dr. Martha Skinner and Dr. Alan Cohen in Boston. Boston University Medical Center had—and still has—a worldwide clearinghouse for information on amyloidosis. From time to time, I'd call the doctors there to inquire of any new developments.

Every day, a new genetic breakthrough seemed to be occurring. Like some Wall Street high-roller following the ups and downs of the market, I scanned the papers and medical journals in search of the latest news. For instance, scientists had made genetic discoveries leading further toward a treatment for Lou Gehrig's disease, which has baffled medical science for a hundred years. I inquired into it, but found it had no application to my genetic disease. At a public event in the governor's reception room, I met the dean of the University of Pittsburgh Medical Center, Dr. George Bernier, Jr. He knew a lot about amyloidosis but gave me little encouragement. I continued to read, continued to ask questions. Why, I don't know, but I felt sure someone or some new breakthrough would deliver me.

In late August 1992, Ellen and I took a nine-day trip to Ireland—just the two of us. It was our first trip to the land of our ancestors. I loved the pristine, unspoiled beauty of Connemara and the West. In Ennis—the seat of County Clare, a 750-year-old town—we even found a little shop with "Casey" emblazoned across it, right near the statue of Daniel O'Connell in the town square.

I was moved by the thought of my ancestors who roamed so far from there, driven by bitter circumstance, by lives much harder than mine had been, and how all those Irish wanderers together had changed America and shaped my own life, character, and faith. I remembered once reading about the Irish warriors who had died in battle, and how they were buried in standing position, facing their enemy. I liked that image, and drew courage from it. As Ellen and I went about our journey, I began to feel weaker and weaker. The symptoms were more obvious on this trip than ever before: stomach distress, waning appetite, nausea. These were unmistakable hints that my own battle was nearing.

With the new year, I could feel myself slipping further. By the spring of 1993, I was having dizzy spells. Getting out of a car or an airplane, often with reporters and cameramen watching, the dizziness—a kind of lightheadedness—would hit me. My blood was by now pooling at the bottom of my feet with each long stretch of sitting. When I stood up, I'd have to get my bearings. I began inventing excuses for the few seconds I needed to allow the dizziness to pass. I'd stop, turn to my staff, and say, "Let me see that schedule," or some other excuse. I even asked Ellen to travel with me, to help with such moments. When a reporter would ask, "How are you feeling, Governor?" I always had a stock answer ready: "I'm fine. How are *you* feeling?" Since I was functioning without any difficulty, I became impatient with questions like that, although they were understandable.

I was steadily losing weight too. Small abrasions weren't healing. The dizziness continued. And I didn't know it, but my heart was defying all medical odds. Doctors later told me it shouldn't have been pumping at all.

With campaign-like intensity, I began to canvass the doctors and contacts I'd been writing and calling since my diagnosis. I still refused to accept the verdict that nothing could be done to cure my condition. With every spare moment, I read, called, listened, searched. The doctors at Boston University told me about a liver transplant surgeon in Boston who had performed a small number of experimental liver transplants for some sufferers of another strain of familial amyloidosis which ravaged its victims in their thirties, leaving them wheelchair-bound because of problems in their legs. Unlike my strain, theirs did not affect the heart.

Excited, I called the transplant surgeon, Dr. David Lewis, who had trained at the University of Pittsburgh under Dr. Thomas Starzl, a world-renowned transplant surgeon. We talked for over an hour. The patients were doing well, he said. Some improvement in their symptoms, but it was still only a few months after their surgery. "If successful, would surgery get rid of the residual amyloid in a patient's system?" I asked him. He couldn't say whether or not it would.

The same day, he faxed me a copy of his article describing the procedure and the improved symptoms of the patients. He also included a copy of *The Lancet,* an international medical journal that reported on some familial amyloidosis liver transplants performed in Sweden beginning in 1990. Some of the cases seemed to involve my strain, and I devoured the article. The case of a Swedish business executive was especially encouraging. In his sixties, he was able to continue to travel all over the world after his surgery.

I immediately told Ellen about the article and called my doctors at Hershey Medical Center. Of course, Ellen cautioned me not to get my hopes up just yet. She didn't want me to be disappointed later. But with every new scientific breakthrough that made news, somebody out there knew one more thing that could make a difference. "With all the things being done every new day with gene therapy," I told her, "there's got to be something out there for me. Somebody out there, somewhere, knows something about this."

My political life had always been a series of long shots. Often it seemed like I had to do everything the hard way. Nothing was ever a sure thing. Always difficult, always a roll of the dice. Here, too, I could feel it. Things would turn around. Something was going to turn up.

That "something" came in a coincidental phone call, the first in a chain of little miracles that saved my life.

4

A Gift

*Faith for him was like the fresh air outside a coal mine—
something he'd breathed in throughout his life and
appreciated more than most men, without ever really thinking much about it.*

ANYONE who has ever been really ill knows that feeling of isolation I
have described. You're there in a crowd of people, and yet not quite
there. Others may give you all the time and care they have to give. But
you feel adrift, cut loose, pulled away. It can be terribly lonely. But if
there is one good thing about such moments, it's that they bring the
mind back to basics. During the period after learning of my illness, I
was beginning to think more about my faith.

All my adult life, I'd found inspiration and strength in my father's life.
In difficult times I always thought of him—what he would say, what he
would do. His life had been an example set before me of what it was to
work hard, persevere, and be unselfish even amid your own struggles.
Now I found myself thinking more about the faith that inspired him.
What was his source of strength?

My parents didn't talk much about their faith, and I've never been one
to do so either. I saw my parents living it, enacting their beliefs in all they
did. For my parents, faith was just the theme of their everyday lives.

My mother, Marie Cummings Casey, was the woman who would do

the jobs with the town's charities that no one else wanted. She was the one who went door to door for the United Way, for instance. She was generous to all. I remember a poor old man who would knock on our door asking for money. Mother would always give it to him. One day, she read in the newspaper that the man had died. She went to the funeral home. There she found that he had no family, no pall bearers, nothing. So she went out and bought him a suit of clothes to be buried in. Later that day, she attended his funeral; she was the only person at the service.

As a lawyer, my father was always helping people down on their luck. If you asked him why, he'd never have said: "Because it is our duty to help others." Helping others just seemed his way, the natural reflex of someone who knew what it was like to need a break. Faith for him was like the fresh air outside a coal mine—something he'd breathed in throughout his life and appreciated more than most men, without ever really thinking much about it. He wasn't what you'd call a pious person. But he had that quiet understanding about life and people that comes with faith. Even if he seldom spoke of it, faith made him the man he was.

My father was the only hero I ever had growing up. When I was governor, enjoying triumphs and comforts and applause that he had never enjoyed, I only admired him all the more deeply. Like thousands of turn-of the-century American immigrant sons, Dad began his life in those mines. Somehow he always pressed on. A natural optimism coupled with a fierce determination allowed him to realize his dream of becoming a lawyer, the first member of my family to complete his education and enter a profession.

My father had to grow up quickly. His father had died young and then one day his mother went into the hospital for a routine operation and never came home. Even though he was the second oldest and still a teenager, it fell to him to be leader of the family and breadwinner for his brothers and sisters. Faced with such a situation, the average person—especially one so young—would feel compelled to quit school. Not my dad. He dropped out of school to work, all right—and then dropped right back in, again and again and again. By the time he finally received his high-school degree, he was in his late twenties.

I've often thought about how embarrassed Dad must have been to sit in a classroom with kids a decade younger than he was. But he saw it through, because it was necessary to reach his goal. He was going to get his education, and that's all there was to it.

A job as a streetcar cleaner and mechanic followed, working down in the grease pits under the cars, and during that time, he became an officer in the Streetcar Men's Union. Fighting for the rights of the workers came natural to him. He was a union man to the core. My brother John and I both remember him talking about the injustices of that day with great passion. He didn't mince words. To him, the Taft-Hartley Law passed by the Congress was the "slave labor law." He was always a fighter, and the rights of workers gave him a cause he could believe in with every fiber of his being.

Among his other jobs, he was a debit man for the Home Life Insurance Company and a pharmaceutical salesman. Then, in his late thirties, he decided it was time to become a lawyer. There was just one problem: He'd never gone to college. In those days, though, Fordham Law School in New York had an admissions program for people who didn't have a college degree but had work histories. In place of the degree, potential candidates were permitted to file what was called "a law students' qualifying certificate." The filing consisted of affidavits from employers attesting to the applicant's good character. If the filing was approved, the applicant was admitted conditionally, and had to stay in good academic standing to remain in school. My father sent to Fordham Law School a stack of affidavits as thick as a "double stack of pancakes," he used to say, because of all the jobs he had held.

He was accepted. But his friends advised against going. He had a good job, they said. He'd have to move, work part-time jobs to live, and could still fail. At his age, why take the chance?

Dad didn't take their advice. He moved to New York, working his way through school as a waiter in the Child's Restaurant chain and finishing Fordham Law School when he as nearly forty years of age. To this day, I have a soft spot in my heart for those who wait on tables in restaurants.

I was born in Jackson Heights, in Queens, New York, January 9, 1932. My father was working at the time for a law firm named Evans, Hunt, and Rees at 220 Broadway. My claim to fame has always been that I was delivered by Dr. Edward Cagney, Jimmy Cagney's brother. Not long afterward, my father and mother moved back to Scranton and he started his own law practice. My mother often recalled for me the day we left New York for Pennsylvania, describing how I laughed as we came across one of the bridges to New Jersey, and of the excitement when we got to Scranton that day.

We moved into a house at 1649 Sanderson Avenue that had been owned by my maternal grandmother until she passed away. It was a big house, but it was packed with family. My brother, John, was born three years later, in 1935. In that house, I lived with my mother and father and younger brother and three of my mother's sisters—one of whom had a family of her own who lived with us. My aunt Lou and my aunt Ann never married. My aunt Margaret married Thomas Jordan, and they had six children. The youngest was Jean (we called her Jeannie) and she had Down's Syndrome.

That living arrangement wasn't all that uncommon in those days, the days of the Depression. Today, with the cost of living the way it is, kids are now doing the same thing. There were very few "empty nests," in any case, back then. Our nest was filled with relatives, young and old.

Life was simple but rich. My mind is full of snapshot images of the life filling each room of that house every hour of the day. In the backyard of that house, there was a cherry tree and a grape arbor. My Uncle Tom raised chickens and tomatoes; both items were regulars on the house menu. He and a friend, Art Meinzer, made sauerkraut down in the cellar in this great, big vat. I can still see them stirring the sauerkraut with a big stick, helped along by a few libations.

Among my most vivid childhood memories were the all-day excursions with my mother on steamy summer days to Rocky Glen amusement park. We traveled to the park on what was called the Laurel Line, an electrified rail line connecting Scranton and Wilkes-Barre with the park located in Moosic, a stop along the way. I was terrified at the sight of the third rail, having been told over and over again about its danger. My mother packed a big lunch full of treats like plums and brownies. We would stay at the park all day and take the Laurel Line back just as night was falling.

My aunt Margaret was always baking bread and pies. Each morning, I'd come down fiddling with my school tie, which I never quite mastered, and there she'd be, kneading the dough with her hands. She would sit me down in a kitchen chair with the flour still on her hands, and she would tie my tie for me. Later at school, I would see that the knot on my tie was white with flour marks.

My father didn't have a car. He never bought one. He took the bus, the streetcar, or would walk everywhere. One of my first memories was walking with my dad, his hand holding mine, to Russell's Ice Cream Store for an ice cream cone. Ice cream on a summer night, trips to Rocky Glen and occasional visits to Atlantic City are among my most cherished memories of those days.

I can see those scarred hands straightening his perfectly-tied necktie, fanning his face with his straw hat, swinging a baseball bat, holding onto a subway strap on our way to a Yankees game, shuffling papers in the court room, and straightening his glasses, always straightening his glasses.

And of course, there were sports. My father loved sports. I remember him with his ear glued to the radio the night Joe Louis beat Billy Conn, the Irish kid from Pittsburgh who would have been the champ had he only stayed away from Louis in the final round. "You're ahead on points!" my dad shouted with millions of other Pennsylvanians that night. "Stay away from him!" To no avail. Conn went in for the KO and paid a heavy price.

As a young man my dad had seen the Four Horsemen of Notre Dame. He would talk about what a great blocker Harry Stuhldreher was, the quarterback in the old Notre Dame box formation and other figures from those glory days of football. We went to fights and ballgames often. Yankee Stadium, Madison Square Garden, the Polo Grounds, old Ebbett's Field in Brooklyn. My dad loved New York because he had gone to school there. We'd stay in the old Taft Hotel

(Vincent Lopez's orchestra played there for what seemed to me forever), and we'd eat in a German restaurant called Steuben's.

I'll never forget one game in Ebbett's Field. Cardinals and Dodgers. The great Stan Musial (born in Donora, Pennsylvania) had been killing the Dodgers at the plate all day. He was four for four, all extra base hits. He came up again in the late innings with two men on base. An elderly gentleman sitting behind us, a rabid Dodger fan, could not bear to see Musial hit again. He said, "I can't take any more of this! I'm leaving." And he walked out.

He was clairvoyant. With the count three and two, Musial hit a fastball over the screen in right field. It was a thrill I'll never forget. Years later, when I was governor, I met Musial and thought of that afternoon at Ebbett's Field with my father when Stan the Man silenced the Dodgers.

When I think about it, our life was the essence of simplicity. There was always enough to eat. We weren't wealthy, but we weren't poor either. Nobody played golf or tennis. We played football in the fall and baseball in the summertime. There was a playground a block-and-a-half away, and that's where we kids spent the summer. It was like a desert in the summer time. But we were kids. What did we care? We'd just pull our shirts off and play ball.

My first brush with right and wrong and my father's style of discipline came when I was about eight. Sanderson Avenue was a very busy street, with a lot of traffic zooming by while I would play outside. One afternoon, for some reason, I picked up a rock and threw it right out into the middle of the road just as a car came along. Of course, the stone crashed into the car's windshield and shattered it with a sickening crunch I can still hear.

I was scared to death and ran around to the back of the house to hide. The owner of the car with the shattered windshield pulled over to the curb, parked, knocked on our door, and went inside. I could hear the sounds of the discussion between the very angry man and my father. I feared the worst as I cowered in the backyard bushes. My father paid for the man's windshield, though, and that was just about it. Dad didn't spank me or discipline me in any way. He just said, "You're not supposed to do that. Don't do it again." There was a gravity in his voice I'd never heard before—I can still hear it, even now.

For my generation time stopped on December 7, 1941. I was sitting on the floor of the living room, playing with some little miniature soldiers, when the grown-ups began talking excitedly about the bombing of Pearl Harbor.

Everything seemed to be different around the neighborhood after that day. There was an electric feeling in the air, the way people looked— and oh, the uniforms. I cherish a picture taken of all of us at a family wedding—my younger brother, Johnny, my mother and father, all my aunts, and all my cousins. My cousin, Henry Jordan, was a navy flier. He married Mary O'Malley and I was an altar boy at the wedding mass. But my awe wasn't reserved for the wedding ceremony. I was taken by his uniform, the dress whites of a naval officer with the gold wings. In my mind, I can still see him standing there posing for that wedding picture with the gold navy wings on his chest.

With the money my father earned from his first big case—a case for the union against the Penn Hat Company that netted him a fee of four thousand dollars (all the money in the world, it seemed at the time)— he bought the house at 2109 Wyoming Avenue not far from Sanderson Avenue which I called home for the rest of my childhood. It is still there, just a block from 2002 North Washington Avenue, where Ellen and I have lived and raised our family since 1962. After I finished my service as governor, we came back to that house on North Washington and live there today.

Because of the difference between our ages, my brother, John, and I had different circles of friends. But growing up we slept in the same room, and like most boys alternated between great squabbles and great fun. Johnny was the mechanical wizard of the house. Anything that was broken, he could repair. He loved to build things, then take them apart and put them back together again. He loved cars, from the little one he drove to local fame and glory in the soap-box derby to the old Bentley he brought home one day from New York City.

He became—no surprise—a mechanical engineer and devotes his considerable talents to his work in the Physical Plant Department at the University of Georgia. He lives today in Athens, Georgia, with his wife, Noleen. Just recently Johnny earned a Ph.D. in Higher Education after years of study. Their daughters, Joleen, Patty, and Mary Elizabeth, are all married now with children of their own.

It was in the house on Wyoming Avenue that I had my first experience with debilitating illness and death. My aunt Lou became so sick she came to live with us. She died in 1952 of breast cancer in our home. I was in college at the time. Lou had been a school teacher all her life. She was one of the most gentle, kind, and loving persons I have ever known.

My aunt Ann worked all her life and never lived anywhere but in her mother's house. Ann Cummings worked as a supervisor at a bank for almost fifty years and was a trusted, valued employee, one of those people you could set your watch by, dependable, loyal, and efficient. When she retired, her pension was something like twelve dollars a month. (My father always said bank employees got the short end of the stick because they didn't organize.) I remember the night she died, in my grandmother's home. She never went to the hospital. She didn't have any health insurance.

This extended family of mine was like any other family. They were ordinary people. They played by the rules. They were neither heroic nor saintly, just decent people with a constancy and quiet stability.

When I think of my mother, the words which come to mind are *generosity* and *civility*. She could not bear to inflict pain or embarrassment on another person. She lived, not for herself, but for others. She seemed to wake up every morning thinking only about what she could do for other people, how she could lighten my father's burden and help her sons, and into what civic "projects" she could throw herself. In return, she asked only that we, too, learn to be considerate of others. It was always "please" and "thank you," and if you forgot to say it, she reminded you. Her influence on me was more subtle, but just as formative, as my dad's.

My father was extremely generous, too, even though he didn't make a lot of money. If anyone had a good excuse to be tight with a dollar, he did. But he never was. He was a soft touch and known for it.

To my knowledge, he had only one regret. I heard him tell the story many times, which was very unlike him. He told it almost like a confession. During the first year or so of his legal career, he was an eyewitness to an accident. A pedestrian had been struck by a car. In spite of himself and against his first impulse, he walked away from the scene.

At the time he had some connection—I can't remember exactly what it was—with an insurance company. He was concerned that he might be called as a witness for the injured pedestrian. So he did not join the other people who rushed to help the victim, and that decision plagued him his whole life. He had such a choice to make once in his life, he'd say, and in his mind he had chosen the wrong course. "If you ever have a similar choice, Bob, don't do that. Don't take the alternative I did."

To my father I owe any victories I've had in life, but also some lessons in how to lose. He ran for public office twice—once for district attorney and once for judge. Both times he ran as an independent in the Democratic primary, always running against the endorsed candidate, bucking the party organization. Both times he lost. In fact, when he ran for district attorney, the party organization actually put up a third candidate named Casey, thereby splitting his vote.

It was a recognition that my father had a constituency; the party organization was taking no chances. He was popular with workers in the Carbondale area, where he had lived and worked as a boy. But he never was embittered by the experience of losing, even when the opposition didn't play by the rules. He remained a loyal Democrat.

As it turned out, his strong showing as a candidate gave me my chance to run for public office. Some of the same party leaders who had opposed him approached me to be the party candidate for the state senate in 1961, probably thinking that a Casey candidacy could now help the whole ticket.

My political career began one day with a phone call. In '61 I was a lawyer practicing in Scranton. One day I was in the courthouse and was called to the telephone. Could I come over to the law office of Richard P. Conaboy, the Democratic county chairman? Over I went. To my surprise, there was Commissioner Michael F. Lawler, the man who ran the party in Lackawanna County (and a shirt-tail relative on my mother's side) sitting with Conaboy. I had a strong sponsor in County Judge William J. Nealon, who had been the Democratic chairman before Conaboy and was a close adviser to Lawler. Judge Nealon's family and mine had known each other for years. He knew my father well and reminded Lawler that my dad had a strong following in the county which would be helpful to me and the other candidates.

"How would you like to run for the open Senate seat, Bob?" Lawler said. "It doesn't look like there'll be a primary fight."

I almost fell off my chair in surprise. But the prospect had strong appeal to me. After talking it over with Ellen, I called the next day and accepted the offer. The strong support from Nealon and Conaboy, both of whom went on to become respected federal judges, secured my selection. I won the election, my first office, and was on my way.

My dad died before I was admitted to the bar. He missed it by two months. My dream was to come back to Scranton and practice with him. Instead, when he died in 1956, I moved home for awhile to help wind up the affairs of his office, including some of his pending cases.

That was how I found myself standing in front of the Pennsylvania Supreme Court to argue my first case, one of Dad's. It was before I was admitted to practice before the Supreme Court. I was twenty-six years old. Needless to say, I was apprehensive. But it was an interesting case, the quintessential Alphonsus L. Casey suit: *Thomas* v. *the Trustees of the Anthracite Health and Welfare Fund.*

A man named Thomas brought an action against the trustees who administered the Miner's Pension Fund. They had taken away his pension and we were trying to get it back. For years, Thomas, a retired miner, went into the fund's office in downtown Scranton to make the payment necessary to maintain his eligibility for pension benefits. One day, the clerk behind the counter told him, "You're all paid up. You don't have to pay anymore." So he followed the instruction and didn't make any more payments.

When the time came for him to receive his pension, you can probably guess what happened. "Sorry," he was told. "You're not eligible. You didn't keep up your payments."

Thomas found a champion in my father, who filed suit on his behalf against the trustees to recover his pension. The Lackawanna County Court had ruled in favor of Thomas shortly before my father died.

The trustees decided to appeal. I worked on the brief with one of my father's colleagues, Myron Pinkus, then prepared to argue—in the highest court in our state—my very first case.

Since I wasn't admitted to practice yet in the Pennsylvania Supreme Court, I asked Pinkus to appear with me to "move my admission" for purposes of that one case.

I remember approaching the lectern at which lawyers stood to present their arguments to the court. There was a satin pillow on it, and I put the palms of my hands on the pillow because they were wet with perspiration. The adrenaline was pumping. I took a deep breath and began.

My father always told me that *facts* win cases. So I began my argument by saying, "I represent Mr. Thomas. He worked in the anthracite coal mines for fifty years. Now they want to take away his pension. . . ."

Justice Michael Musmanno, a well-known advocate for the underdog, was a member of the court. He interrupted me almost immediately. "Counsel, will you repeat what you just said? Did I understand you to say that this man worked in the anthracite coal mines for fifty years, and now they want to take away his pension?"

"That's correct, Your Honor."

"Fifty years!" his voice intoned incredulously.

At that moment, I knew we'd won the case.

When my argument was finished, Chief Justice John C. Bell, Jr., a former Pennsylvania governor, said to me as I left the podium, "I want to compliment you on presenting a fine argument." You can imagine how I felt as a rookie hearing such plaudits from the bench. (Come to think of it, that was the first and only time it ever happened!) The only thing that would have made the moment more satisfying would have been for my father to stand there with me. But that was not to be.

I had to appear in Pittsburgh during the court's next term to be admitted to the Bar of the Pennsylvania Supreme Court. The admissions ceremony was a cut and dried affair, impersonal. There was one motion filed by the clerk of the Supreme Court on behalf of the dozens of young lawyers, including me, who were in the court room to be admitted.

What a difference it would have made if my father could have been there to make the motion for admission on behalf of his son. But he was there, in spirit. I could almost feel his presence as I returned to my seat and the court began to announce decisions in cases which had been argued during the previous term. Justice Musmanno announced the Court's decision in the case of *Thomas* v. *The Trustees of the Anthracite Health and Welfare Fund*. "The judgment in favor of the plaintiff is affirmed."

We had won. Hearing those words, I was euphoric. And I said to myself, "This one's for you, Dad!"

The tough times in life force you to reach far back, deep inside yourself to find something permanent, solid, to hold onto. My father, his spirit, his ways, his courage, his whole attitude toward life, has always been there for me whenever I've reached back. And the quiet, constant encouragement and support I had received from my mother gave me the strength I needed to keep going, despite the setbacks. During my sickness I began to see how much faith in God had guided them through life, and touched my own life just as quietly. It wasn't such a "natural" reflex at all: It was a gift we'd received. My whole life was a gift. The man and woman who gave me life and raised me were a gift. My faith was a gift. Now, I realized, I needed faith more than ever. To be strong, I needed to be weak enough to acknowledge my complete dependence upon it. And maybe for the first time, I was truly grateful.

Modern man has not lost faith, someone had said, "but we have transferred it from God to the medical profession." I needed both—faith in God, and faith in the skill and wisdom of men. But more important, I began to see how much those two went together.

When I lost my mother and father, I took great consolation in the faith they had nurtured in me—especially in the words of the funeral Mass which said that "life is changed, not ended" by death, so that I was not saying a final good-bye but rather "'Til we meet again."

5

Little Miracles

*... I felt like a man deep in quicksand who had just felt
a strong hand take hold of his wrist.*

THE SPRING and summer of 1993 brought me what I can only
describe as a string of miracles, blessed coincidences coming together
to save my life. A passing conversation. A persistent friend. A gift book.
A random call. A last-moment question. A legislative drama. An act of
violence redeemed into an act of staggering generosity.

It began in April, when State Treasurer Catherine Baker Knoll called
me on business. As we wrapped up our work, she said in passing, "By
the way, have you seen the book from Dr. Starzl?"

"What book?" I answered. A renowned Pittsburgh transplant surgeon
named Thomas Starzl had inscribed a copy of his autobiography, *The
Puzzle People: Memoirs of a Transplant Surgeon,* and sent it to me, and
Catherine wanted to make sure I'd seen it.

I had never met Dr. Starzl but I knew him by reputation. He was one
of those people who pushed the envelope in medicine to spectacular
and often controversial results. I told Catherine I'd check into it. And I
intended to: Maybe there was something there about amyloidosis. But
somehow the whole thing slipped my mind.

Weeks went by. May arrived. When I think back and piece the story together, one day during that period seems especially remarkable. I had just conducted "Capital for a Day" in Donora, in the hard-hit southwestern part of Pennsylvania. "Capital for a Day" was a program in which I packed up my entire cabinet and traveled to one of Pennsylvania's towns for two full days of town meetings and give-and-take with anyone and everyone who wanted to ask questions or air grievances.

There was just one rule for the town meetings: We stayed until we had heard every questioner. Sometimes we stayed past midnight. We'd finished the program in Donora and proceeded to nearby Monessen, the town where I'd spent my first day in office vowing to bring economic development to the region. We were returning to give awards to several single parents who had moved from welfare to work through one of our programs called "New Directions." The ceremony took place in the building where many of the ravaged steel town's people had received recent job training, and among them was a young man named William Michael Lucas.

That was as close as I would come to meeting Michael Lucas, the young man whose life six weeks later would come together with mine.

The weeks after that visit to Monessen dissolved into a blur of meetings, speeches, interviews, dedications, and travel—almost constant travel. I wasn't at the top of my game, and probably looked much worse than I felt.

Then on May 11, after a morning speech at the National Press Club in Washington, I flew back to a Pepperidge Farms Baking facility in Pennsylvania's Lancaster County. We were filming an economic-development commercial there. We'd already filmed for over an hour inside the plant, and now I was scheduled to be taken by van to a parking lot, where I would pose beside a helicopter flown in just for the filming. As I stepped up to enter the van, something happened.

I'd done it millions of times before. But this time, when I raised my leg to enter the van, I slipped and gashed my right shin on the step's metal edge. Blood rushed out of the wound. The trooper with me managed to wrap a bandage around it, stopping the blood flow for the moment.

Meanwhile, a crew of television production people were standing outside in the oppressive heat, waiting for the "star" to make his appearance. The only thing to do was go ahead. We did three takes with me standing there in a blood-soaked shoe, offering a hearty, "Welcome to Pennsylvania!" In the last of these shots, I had to simulate getting into the helicopter, eagerly departing on some unspecified mission. I approached the chopper, turning to the camera with a happy wave. They took the shot, and from there I was driven straight to Hershey Medical Center, where I received six stitches.

The next morning, Ellen and I were scheduled to make an appearance on behalf of the Children's Health Insurance Program (CHIP)—one of our new programs—at a neighborhood health center in Harrisburg. CHIP provided free or low-cost healthcare to children. It was a very generous program, covering a wide range of services for poor children, and I was quite proud of it.

The wound had not closed during the night, but the next morning, we went to the center anyway. As I began my remarks, I could again feel blood running down into my shoe. I tried to distract myself from it, focusing on my words and the children before me—but it was no use. By the time I'd finished my speech, my shoe was soaked. "We'd better go home," I said to Ellen.

At home, Ellen changed the bandage and urged that we head back to the hospital. Finally, after completing another event at a playground in Harrisburg, I agreed. At the hospital, I received several more stitches. I returned to the hospital four more times that month because the nasty gash refused to heal. When I asked doctors why the wound wouldn't heal, the response was "venous changes" in the leg. That sounded authoritative enough, so I didn't inquire further. It was troublesome but not disabling, and I really didn't want to know the details.

Soon, however, there were more bad signs. The same month Ellen and I flew to see our youngest son, Matt, graduate from Notre Dame. We would also attend his Phi Beta Kappa induction, and I was to receive an honorary degree. But the first morning of the trip, I awoke as tired as I'd ever been—just done in.

Ellen and I had prided ourselves on attending every game, every recital, every first communion—in fact, every important event in the lives of our children. That morning I could hardly stand up, much less put in a day of walking, speaking, and meeting people. "I don't think I can make the induction ceremony," I told Ellen. We agreed she should go without me. Quietly closing the door behind her, she told our son, "Dad needs to rest." Matt told me later that he didn't like the sound of that. The next day, I sat on the stage as Matt received his Notre Dame degree. And the college conferred an honorary degree on me. But walking down a long hallway after the ceremony, I felt myself getting dizzy and had to stop until my head cleared.

To make matters worse, I was losing not only energy but appetite. This had never before been a problem. Now, suddenly, I could hardly bear the thought of a full meal. I didn't understand until later but I was beginning to feel the effects of malnutrition, as the protein fibrils caused by amyloidosis piled up in my system. It got so bad that when Ellen and I entertained dinner guests that spring, I had to pretend I had eaten an earlier meal to avoid questions, when in fact all I had eaten was a handful of raw carrots.

It was Catherine Baker Knoll who inadvertently came to my rescue. As an afterthought during a working phone call that May, she again asked if I'd seen the book by Dr. Starzl. "You know, I'd completely forgotten about that." This time I followed up. Immediately I called my assistant, Bonnie Seaman. "Bonnie, did I receive a book from Dr. Thomas Starzl?"

We had a standard procedure for gifts. Under our ethics law, we documented and appraised each item before accepting it. The book was catalogued somewhere in that pipeline, and within minutes I had it in hand. The inscription read:

> To Governor Robert P. Casey with admiration for your efforts to improve healthcare in our state of Pennsylvania.
> —Tom Starzl
> PS: I hope to meet you sometime in the future.
> —T.S.

A few minutes later, I had Dr. Starzl on the line to thank him for the gift. I hardly remember how the conversation began, but I'll never forget how it ended. On the spur of the moment, just as Dr. Starzl was saying good-bye, I asked, "By the way, what do you know about familial amyloidosis?"

"I'll call you back in five minutes."

I hung up the phone and waited. In five minutes, it rang. "Governor, I can *cure you* with a liver transplant."

He said "cure." No qualifiers. No ifs, no ands, no buts. A *cure*.

I can't even remember how I responded to those words, but I know it was one of the happiest moments of my life. For some reason—perhaps something I just sensed about this man—I believed him. I had no doubts at all.

Immediately I called home. "I've found it, Ellen. Tom Starzl says he can *cure* me!"

I know what that must have sounded like to her. She feared I might be reaching for a rope of sand, that the eventual let-down might only make things worse. "Don't get your hopes up, Spike," she said gently, using my nickname from basketball days. "Let's find out more about this, okay?"

That night I turned the conversation with Starzl over and over in my mind, still hopeful but now examining the risks of a transplant in the calm light of reason. I took a yellow legal pad and drew up two columns—"Risks" and "Benefits." It didn't take long until the exercise seemed absurd. Under "Benefits," I wrote simply: "Can't get any worse." That settled it.

The next morning my assistant, Bonnie, handed me the package Dr. Starzl had promised to send. There, on top, was a letter repeating, with no disclaimers, no hedging whatsoever, his assurance that he could cure me. I'd been delivered. Reading and rereading that letter, I felt like a man deep in quicksand who had just felt a strong hand take hold of his wrist.

When I told Dr. Graham Jeffries, my internist, about Dr. Starzl's assurance to me, he said, "You know, Governor, Dr. Starzl is an optimist."

"You know, Dr. Jeffries," I answered, "So am I."

6

Pure Luck

It was one of those beautiful spring days, a bright, crisp spring day to greet our child.

EVEN AT low points in life I have always counted myself the luckiest of men. Lots of setbacks along the way, but lucky when it really counted. From the start I was blessed with a strong and loving family.

By high school, I was attending Scranton Prep, a Jesuit high school which opened in 1944. Classes were small. *Too* small: there was no place to hide. I was called on every day by teachers like Father Paul Reed, who introduced himself at the beginning of the school year this way: "The more you guys hate me, the better I like it. Get a good night's sleep tonight. It'll be your last until June." He was not kidding. I found myself hitting the books for three to four hours—every night.

I met Ellen about that time. We were both fourteen. She was the most beautiful girl I ever saw, then or since. And she was as good as she looked—a good person through and through. Forty-three years of marriage have only left me in greater awe of her goodness.

God was never more kind to me than on the day I first saw her, though at first I felt forsaken: When I had finally worked up the nerve to ask her out, I didn't even do the asking. I couldn't, since we hadn't really met. I asked her cousin, Pete O'Donnell, to do it for me. Pete, a pal of mine, called Ellen, and I listened on the extension phone.

"Want to go to the prom with my friend, Spike Casey?" I heard him ask.

"No," she answered.

That was that. She said she already had a date.

I've always told her that was her first big mistake. Of course, what I *didn't* tell her was that I never got around to asking anyone else to the prom, and wound up working in the cloak room. But she knew anyway. Ellen told me she made a point of strolling by the cloak room that night to check me out.

I guess I passed inspection because the next time I was brave enough to ask her for a date, months later, she said yes.

We used to meet each other at the YMCA dances every Friday night. All the girls gathered at one end of the room and all the boys congregated at the other. After the dance, I'd walk her home. My brother, John, likes to remind me how deep true love went, since I would actually take nighttime shortcuts through a nearby cemetery to visit her. She lived on the other side.

Luck was with me again as I was about to graduate. College was just months away. I'd been a pretty good basketball player in high school, but was actually a better baseball player. Mike O'Neill, the local scout for the Philadelphia Phillies, once asked my dad if he wanted to discuss my signing a pro contract. But my journey to Cooperstown was cut short when Holy Cross intervened and I turned to basketball. Out of sheer happenstance, I was given a tryout with the college's basketball team.

Though a small liberal arts college, in those days Holy Cross was the place to be if you were a basketball player. The school had won the NCAA National Basketball Championship in 1947 and had produced some of the sport's legends, including Bob Cousy. Cousy was a consensus all-American and was inducted into the Basketball Hall of Fame, as was Tommy Heinsohn, another Holy Cross great during my time there. Two other all-Americans at Holy Cross were Earle Markey, my class-mate and good friend, and Togo Palazzi. Kareem Abdul Jabbar—back when he was known as Lew Alcindor—even visited Holy Cross as a high-school player years later, its reputation as a basketball power still intact.

Holy Cross offered six freshman basketball scholarships that year. Five had already been given. They had held a jamboree-type tryout weekend to which they invited hundreds of basketball hopefuls from across the country. From that huge group, five emerged and were of-fered scholarships. I can guarantee if I'd gone through that jamboree process, I never would have been one of the five.

But Holy Cross had one slot left. The competitive process was over. It was late in the year. I think they were getting a little desperate. One of the Jesuit priests at my high school called the athletic director at Holy Cross and said, "We have this kid. He's a pretty good ball player, and I think you ought to take a look at him."

"Fine," the athletic director said. "Send him up."

So, over Easter weekend, I was to have my tryout. My father and I boarded the train in Scranton and went to Hoboken, and there, de-scended the steps to the "Hudson tubes" that stretched beneath the Hudson River to New York City. Then, from Grand Central Station, we took a Pullman sleeper car all the way to Worcester, Massachu-setts. This was very impressive for a small-town boy. We boarded the train in New York at night and woke up on a siding the next morning in Worcester. I remember pulling up the Eisenglass curtain and see-ing that we were literally "parked" in the railroad yard of the train station.

By then, it was Sunday morning. We hailed a cab and rode to the Holy Cross gymnasium, where two men were waiting. One of these two was the coach, Lester "Buster" Sheary.

Buster Sheary was an old football player who went on to coach basket-ball without ever pausing to notice the differences between the two. He thought like a football player, acted like a football player, and coached like a football player. He was a product of the boys clubs and the sandlots, the rough-and-tumble semi-pro sports scene in Massachusetts. And he was a blood-and-guts, knock-'em-down, hit-'em-again, don't-pick-'em-up type of coach. That was his philosophy. He loved contact, and his basketball teams played that way. One week during practice, one of the players received a concussion and another suffered a broken nose. Buster looked especially proud that week: His boys were finally learning to play *real* basketball!

So my dad and I walked in, suitcase in hand, to find Buster Sheary pacing around the gym. Next to him was a formidable figure named James O'Neil, introduced to me as "Shuffles."

O'Neil was six-feet-four and weighed about 235 with "zero" body fat. He was a big kid from Ohio, and a tremendous athlete. Shuffles was loose as a goose, free and easy. No one had to ask Shuffles to lighten up. He played on both the Holy Cross basketball and baseball teams, pitching three consecutive winning games in the college world series for our '52 NCAA National Championship Baseball team. He had a fastball with a major-league hop on it. It looked like an aspirin tablet coming in. There was no mystery about what Shuffles was going to serve up. It was going to be that fastball. "Come on—try and hit it," he'd say. Most guys couldn't even see it, let alone hit the thing.

In basketball, his gift was rebounding. He had no fear. He didn't know his own strength. He was so strong that guys would bounce off him without his ever breaking stride. But Shuffles was also a bit eccentric. He'd disappear for days, then reappear in the gym in the dead of winter with a duffel bag and no overcoat.

So there was Shuffles standing quietly by Buster Sheary, waiting for me. What I didn't know was that Coach Sheary was looking for a rebounder. The player he needed had to be able to go up and come down with the ball, just like Shuffles. Maybe he couldn't shoot, maybe he couldn't dribble, maybe he couldn't pass, but he had to be strong enough to go up and take the ball off the backboard. Sheary proceeded on the general theory that you couldn't score if you didn't have the ball, so the name of the game was always, "Get the ball."

"That's our ball up there," I can still hear exhorting us before each practice. "If it's on the floor, it's our ball. If it's off the backboard, it's our ball. You wake up in the morning and say, 'What's the first rule? Get the ball!'" So that day he wanted to see if I could—get the ball.

My tryout consisted of Buster Sheary taking the ball and throwing it up at the basket so Shuffles and I could wrestle, bang, elbow, push, or knock each other around to get the ball. Shuffles banged me around the whole time, but somehow I got the ball often enough to convince Coach Sheary that maybe if he brought me on the team, I could get the ball for him.

Besides that, everything I shot went in. Any basketball player knows that some days the basket has a lid on it. But not that morning. It was one of those days you dream about. I have lived on the memory of that morning ever since. Couldn't miss.

Whatever happened in Buster's gym that day was enough to get me the scholarship to Holy Cross, and I showed up the following September. That day of my tryout was probably the high point of my whole basketball career, I have to admit. I have never played like that before or since. From there, it was all downhill. After my starting berth on the freshman team, I was a bench warmer on the varsity for three years.

I remember best the moments I was on the court with Bob Cousy. He was a senior while I was a freshman. He was an icon in the making—a genius with a basketball. He wasn't that tall, but he had an incredible physique for basketball—his arms hung way below his belt. He had narrow, sloping shoulders, was deceptively fast, moved like a cobra, and could palm a basketball like it was a tennis ball. He would move down the floor with this fluid motion. Freshmen players—including me—would play against him every night in practice.

Our freshman team provided cannon fodder for Cousy and the rest of the varsity team at these practices. We were the skins and they were the shirts. We played them tough every night. But this team, loaded with great players, was the one that set a new intercollegiate record for consecutive victories in 1950—twenty-six victories in a row—and was ranked Number One nationally that year. We freshmen could barely keep up with the third-string team.

What I remember most about Cousy was that he was always the first guy on the court at night, refining his moves a hundred times before practice even started. He'd perfected one maneuver that many of the players execute now, even kids, but one we'd never seen before. He'd fire down the court at full speed until he hit the foul line where he'd literally go airborne toward the basket, flip the ball behind his back, then put it through the basket with the opposite hand. He was so deceptive, he'd embarrass the players on his own team. He'd pass the ball without looking at them and hit them in the head. His skill was rivaled by none and his desire to win was awesome. There was no such thing as a "practice" game. Every scrimmage was a game. He was a fiery competitor and a man of integrity who would in later years quit coaching basketball because he was put off by what he regarded as the excesses of the game. And while the rest of us didn't have the skill of a Bob Cousy, we were expected at every practice to have the same heart and drive.

Holy Cross also gave me my first taste of close-call political defeat. I ran for class president as a freshman and lost the election by four votes. All four came from the infirmary. I was learning my political lessons early—always work on those absentee ballots and never take one vote for granted. When I ran successfully for senior class president in my first political comeback, I worked the infirmary hard.

My four years at Holy Cross whizzed by in a blur of turning textbook pages and long nights spent studying. Scholarship athletes had to keep up with their school work—no allowances made. We practiced for two or three hours every night during the season, and often returned late on game nights. We were still expected to be in class bright and early the next morning.

I was in the A/B Honors course at Holy Cross—a fairly rugged routine. The load of Latin and Greek required in the program only added to the difficulty.

Ellen and I didn't see much of each other during those years except on holidays or special events at school. She flew to Logan Airport in Boston for our junior prom. I didn't have a car so I borrowed one from a classmate, Art Frawley, and went to pick her up. I arrived at the airport all dandied up in a suit and new straw hat—a "skimmer," we called it. Somehow the moment stands out in memory—the happiness of our reunion, driving along together on a beautiful, bright spring day on the way back from Boston for the prom.

Despite the straw hat, Ellen agreed to marry me. We became man and wife on June 27, 1953, two weeks after we finished college. We had our wedding reception in Ellen's grandmother's house on Jefferson Avenue. All our friends from Holy Cross and Marywood, Ellen's college, were there. The only sad note was the absence of Ellen's older brother Ray Harding, who was serving in Korea in the army. I didn't have a job and was scheduled to start law school the following September. I had been accepted to the University of Pennsylvania Law School. But I was worried about being able to afford the tuition.

One day I was going up the steps in one of the main buildings at Holy Cross and happened to spot a notice on the big bulletin board, an ad announcing the George Washington University Trustee Scholarship Program. The board of trustees gave two scholarships each year to the law school. To apply, a prospective candidate simply sent in a résumé attached to a copy of his transcript. I applied immediately. Within a few weeks, I had an interview with an alumnus of the law school who lived in Worcester, and that was it. Lucky again, I received an all-tuition scholarship to the George Washington University Law School.

We packed up and headed for Washington, D.C., where we lived for about a month with Ellen's uncle, Gene Butler, and his family at Number 8 East Melrose Street, just above Chevy Chase Circle. The high-rent district. Soon, though, we had found an apartment in the southeastern part of the city, in a garden-type apartment development called "Skyland."

The rent was fifty-seven dollars a month. Soon Ellen became pregnant with our first child. That fact, of course, meant there would be no tranquil days of study as I prepared for my law career: I would have to find a job. I sold World Book encyclopedias door to door, and that job lasted for an entire week. Didn't sell one book. Delivered from this humiliating vocation, I landed part-time work at the District of

Columbia Public Library at Seventh and New York Avenue. The building is still there, but all boarded up now. In those days, it was square in the middle of the "Tenderloin District." There were burlesque shows across the street and men lying around on newspapers on park benches. The library was a public building, so poor souls would come in to warm up in the winter and stay cool in the summer. My job was shelving books part-time, and my pay was a king's ransom of twenty-six dollars a week.

We didn't go hungry, though. A charge account with Thompson's Dairy helped that. Home delivery was then a normal service—eggs, milk, butter. We were well-nourished, consuming more than our share of dairy products during those days on the cuff until the end of the month.

I didn't work at the library too long. Soon, one of my law school professors—Forrester Davison, who taught administrative law—helped me get a job as a part-time law clerk at the prestigious firm of Covington & Burling, located in the Union Trust Building at Fifteenth and H Streets, NW. My paycheck went from twenty-six dollars a week to fifty dollars a week, just like that. Life was good.

Then on April 13, 1954, our first child was born in Doctor's Hospital in Washington. Her name was Margaret, named after Ellen's mother, and she entered this world at 7:28 A.M. It was one of those beautiful spring days, a bright, crisp spring day to greet our child. All cares of final exams and paychecks faded away at the wonder of that day. I was the luckiest man on earth. I'll never forget the first time I saw her. The nursery had the shade pulled down over the two large windows. I just stood at the window, waiting. All of a sudden the nurse raised the shade and there she was, with a pink ribbon around her one little curl— a brand-new life the world had never seen before.

7

Last Rites

That was the only way to go about this whole thing. I would proceed on the assumption of full recovery, and as many years to come as God would give me.

WE HAVE *to move quickly*. That was my first thought after the excitement of Dr. Starzl's promised cure.

I sensed that time was very short. An old friend of mine, State Senator Frank Lynch, had just died of a terminal illness, and I think that sobered me even as I suddenly seemed to be rushing toward a cure. In a way, Frank may have helped save my own life with his final act.

An early budget is very rare in any state, but we were able to get the budget passed ahead of schedule in 1993. On May 28, after finishing "Capital for a Day" in Hazelton, I hopped a plane to Harrisburg. We were expecting the final budget vote that day. Had the vote not come, things would likely have dragged on, perhaps preventing me from receiving the immediate medical treatment I needed.

To cast the deciding vote, Frank was carried into the Senate Chamber on a stretcher. I had called him from Hazelton that morning to thank him for his heroics, not really understanding at the time what it meant for me. By midnight, I had signed the budget, and five days later I found myself attending Frank's funeral.

It was agreed that my doctors would meet in Pittsburgh with Dr. Starzl and Dr. John Fung, a renowned surgeon in his own right and the University of Pittsburgh Medical Center's transplant division chief. A meeting was set for Tuesday, June 8, in a room at Pittsburgh's William Penn Hotel. Present were Dr. Starzl and Dr. Fung, Doctors Leaman and Jeffries of the Hershey Medical Center, Brian Broznick, the head of an organization called CORE—the organ procurement organization for western Pennsylvania—Ellen and I.

"Before we get started," I began, "I just want to tell you this. I know there is a process, a book of rules, that governs the allocation of organs for transplantation. I am telling you right now that you must assure me— each of you—that all of these rules will be followed in my case. I want a guarantee before we say another word that the same rules will apply to me that would apply to a steel worker from McKeesport if he needed an organ transplant. Whatever the process is, you will follow it to the letter."

All agreed. Now it was their turn to speak.

Dr. Leaman said, "The governor's heart is too weak to withstand a liver transplant."

Dr. Leaman had brought my medical records from Hershey and reviewed some of the contents with the other doctors.

The decision was made to bring me to Pittsburgh for an evaluation on the prospects of a liver transplant. At that point, neither Dr. Starzl nor any other doctor in Pittsburgh had ever examined me or taken any tests. An evaluation would include tests designed to see whether my heart was strong enough to withstand a liver transplant. If not, then a heart-liver transplant would have to be considered.

Dr. Fung and Dr. Starzl also explained that if a double transplant became necessary, both organs would have to be transplanted in successive operations on the same day, and both organs would have to come from the same donor.

No medical decisions were made that day except to go forward as soon as possible with the evaluation—the tests which would determine the final course of action.

"I'd like you to go directly to the University of Pittsburgh Medical Center today to be admitted so we can begin," Dr. Starzl told me.

"I can't do that," I said. "I can't just suddenly appear at the hospital. I'd have to hold a press conference about any sort of hospital visit, especially one that might end up in something as serious as a transplant operation. I have to explain what we've decided to do and why we decided to do it. And you all should be there, especially Dr. Starzl," I told the group. That meant we had to wait a few more days, like it or not. We spent the rest of the meeting working out our mutual schedules.

Afterward I sent one of my aides to ask Dr. Starzl if I could have a moment alone with him. I wanted him to examine my legs. He checked the pulse in my feet and found almost no circulation in them. At that moment, Dr. Starzl would tell me later, he knew my heart was going to be a problem. A liver transplant alone might not be enough.

On the morning after the meeting with the doctors in Pittsburgh on June 8, 1993, I called the senior staff together to tell them for the first time of the events of the past two weeks and my decision to be evaluated for a liver transplant. It was very unusual for me to summon the staff together upon my arrival in the office. This was the only indication the staff had that I had something important to discuss with them. While we made a few scheduling changes to accommodate my need for additional rest and the trip to Pittsburgh, the daily work of the governor's office went on as usual.

When I told my staff of the events of the prior weeks there was a stunned silence around the table. After the initial shock was over, we had a meeting of several hours to make plans for the press conference on Friday, June 11. Everyone was given assignments to prepare for Friday's announcement and Bonnie Seaman, the most able assistant to any govenor in the Union, was to make the logistical arrangements to have the Pittsburgh and Hershey doctors present.

After a conversation with Dr. Starzl's office, Bonnie told me that Dr. Starzl was in Paris to receive an award from the French Senate. At first, Dr. Starzl's office thought it would be impossible for him to get back to the United States in time for the Friday announcement. They felt that if Dr. Starzl left early, this would cause an international embarrassment and asked if we would consider postponing the press conference until

Monday, June 14. When Bonnie told me about the possible delay, I looked her straight in the eye and said, "Bonnie, I don't have the time to wait." That was the only time I ever verbalized how urgent the situation was. We decided to go back and ask again to see if any exceptional arrangements could be made to get Dr. Starzl back to the United States in time for the press announcement on June 11. That was when it was decided Dr. Starzl would take the Concorde back to be in Harrisburg in time for the press conference.

We held the press conference on Friday, as scheduled. After my statement explaining all I knew and all the hope it offered, we fielded questions from the media.

My statement was upbeat, because that's exactly how I felt: "At last, I've finally been given a chance to fight back against this disease," I said. Dr. Starzl then held court. One reporter asked him, "If the operation is a success, will Governor Casey have a normal life span?"

"We do not guarantee immortality, but I believe it is fair to say that Governor Casey will probably outlive everybody in this room."

That bit of bravado was classic Starzl. He is one of those people who can say such a thing and get away with it—a self-willed man endowed with audacity, but also the genius to back it up. He dared to ignore the accepted wisdom of the day that liver transplantation was too complex, too risky. Advised that liver transplantation couldn't be done, he became an expert in pharmacology, biochemistry, and molecular biology just so that he could prove otherwise. He performed the first successful liver transplant in 1963 at the University of Colorado Medical Center.

Visit his office, and you won't find it in a shiny new high-rise. Among the most acclaimed doctors in the world, Tom Starzl still has his office over a Pizza Hut restaurant in Pittsburgh, and drives there every morning in a sixteen-year-old compact car. You'll never meet a man more free of pretense or self-regard, a person more focused or committed to things beyond himself. He has been a constant, never-say-die advocate for transplantation in all its controversial forms. I knew of the controversy that followed him, and it only made my faith in him that much greater.

That Saturday Ellen and I flew to Pittsburgh for what we thought would be a few days of tests. The moment we left for the hospital, everything seemed to move into fast-forward. A *Pittsburgh Post-Gazette* reporter, Dennis Roddy, had asked to ride with us from the airport into downtown Pittsburgh. We talked about a lot of things, like our recent trip to Ireland, Ellen's cancer ordeal ten years earlier and how we had come through that, about the tests I was about to take, the disease, and about the transplant cure. Then he asked me whether I'd consider returning to politics if such a transplant were successful.

That was a question I'd been asking myself. Granted, it was not the most important question. I would be grateful just to have more time on earth with Ellen and our children. But the question did occur to me, and it probably helped to think about it—to think in terms beyond mere survival. That was the only way to go about this whole thing. I would proceed on the assumption of full recovery, and as many years to come as God would give me. If I made it through this ordeal, what came next would be a sprint and not a victory lap.

Only days before, in a long discussion with Dr. Fung about the operation and the aftermath, he had assured me that I would have a normal life-expectancy if the transplant were successful.

I finally said to him, "All right, Dr. Fung, let me ask you the sixty-four-thousand-dollar question: If the operation is a success, could I be a candidate for public office again, recognizing that a political campaign is the physical equivalent of playing in the National Football League?"

"Absolutely," he answered. "There is nothing that's going to be beyond your capacity if the operation works."

So I told Roddy, as we rode toward a medical ordeal I could not possibly fathom, what I believed deep in my spirit I'd do. "If I can shake this, Dennis, I don't rule anything out."

As our car pulled up to the University of Pittsburgh Medical Center's front doors, the television cameras were everywhere and they were roll-ing. It was a long five yards into that hospital door. I was moving but I wasn't moving too fast. I was relieved to finally be in the hospital's hands. In the last few days, I had noticed a new symptom, a fluttering feeling in my chest.

"Do you want a wheelchair?" someone asked. I waved it off. The press and the cameras were in a fenced-off area near the door. We walked over to the press area and I responded to the barrage of ques-tions. Then we headed to the elevator and the office of cardiologist Dr. William Follansbee. Dr. Follansbee was to become a key player in the long effort to save my life, and then to provide crucial and expert care after my operation. On this day, he would take a medical history as part of the admissions process. The corridor to his office seemed like an interstate highway stretching out of sight.

After the first round of tests, Ellen and our sons Matt and Pat were in the hospital room with me as I ate my evening meal. I remember I had just taken a bite of cheesecake when four of my doctors along with Jef-frey Romoff, the medical center's director, came in. They were back much too quickly.

"Governor," Starzl began, "you are in grave danger of sudden death."

They hadn't gotten any further than the first series of tests. What the test revealed was that my heart was twice its normal weight, with all the suppleness of a medicine ball. I was as close to congestive heart failure as a man could be and still be around to know it. That fluttering I had felt was called atrial fibrillation, a life-threatening symptom. What's more, in this shape my heart would never last through what they called the "insult" of a liver transplant—when blood was flushed through the heart for the first time at the end of the transplant procedure.

It was left to Starzl to deliver the punch line: "You need a heart *and* a liver transplant, and you need them as soon as possible."

Liver transplants were almost common in the medical world; I knew that. Hundreds were done each year, a huge number of them at the University of Pittsburgh Medical Center, and their success rate was an amazing 95 percent. But liver *and* heart transplant? Of the two dozen heart and liver transplants attempted in the world, only six had been in the U.S, and four of those six had been done at the Center. And all four patients were now dead.

"If that's what we have to do," I said, "let's go."

"You are in for the fight of your life, Governor," Starzl said. "But you're going to *win* it."

When he said that, I felt a surge of adrenaline. I had complete confidence that I was going to live. And I had complete confidence in this man, Starzl. I would have followed him through a wall of fire.

And in fact, that was what I was about to do: go through a wall of fire, hoping to find new life on the other side.

I knew that my name had been put on a list. But what Starzl knew that I didn't know was that there was a separate list for heart-liver transplant combinations; and because a heart and liver dual transplant was so rare, I was the only one on that list.

Looking back now, even this deeper plunge into danger seemed a saving grace. My needing a new heart to handle the new liver actually saved my life. If I had been forced to wait the month or more for my name to come to the top of the single transplant list, I probably would have died.

Even at the time, none of these complications shook my conviction that I would survive the surgery. I was convinced, from the first moment Dr. Starzl told me he could cure me with a liver transplant, that I would make it. I remember telling Ellen and the children this before the surgery. "The Lord has carried me this far," I said. "He will carry me the rest of the way."

Doctors later said they gave me a one-in-four chance to live out the week. Even being the only one on the list might not have been enough. Any donated heart and liver still had to be from someone with my build and blood type. And could that happen in time, considering the condition of my heart? I would need at least one more little miracle.

As I sat there in my hospital bed, listening to the doctors and administrators discussing my medical prognosis, I could hear my heart beating. Every beat now was victory over time. And then it struck me: *Stripping away the clinical talk of donor types and waiting lists, what am I actually waiting for? For someone else to die.* For me to live, someone else had to die. Of course it was not a causal connection: These were entirely independent events. Whatever happened would have happened anyway. But it still was not a comforting thought. On the grand scale, it would take somebody else's tragedy to tip the balance in my favor.

Only later would I hear about the behind-the-scenes controversy among the medical center staff that night. I was too old, too sick, went one view. The odds were too long. To do two transplants on me was incredibly risky—for many reasons. Surgery on the governor of the state in this situation might look like medical grandstanding, favoritism.

And that was the best case. In the worst case—if the operation failed—before the eulogies were done there would be a flurry of criticism and second-guessing about the waste of two precious organs. If the team of surgeons failed, they failed in a big way, and they failed publicly. And if they succeeded, the media would dissect every aspect of each decision anyway. That was the raw truth, and exactly what would happen.

But Starzl wouldn't hear it. He believed new techniques and new drugs would make the difference. "Besides," he told the doubters, "The governor's a fighter."

Those doctors who weren't convinced, Starzl promptly removed from the transplant team. As he later told *Reader's Digest,* "If you're going on an expedition to the South Pole, you don't want someone coming along who isn't sure you're going to make it."

Meanwhile, my deputy chief of staff, Jack Tighe, was busy setting up a "governor's office" in the hospital. We had known when I went into the hospital that I might have to relinquish my duties to the lieutenant governor at some point. But we had thought this trip was just for tests and that I'd be able to continue my duties from my hospital bed. Now, it looked like we were in for a long wait. I asked Jack to have my press secretary, Vince Carocci, prepare a press release. Then we set up a conference call with the rest of my family except for Chris, who was not reachable by phone.

"Well, I've got some late-breaking news for you," I told everyone. Between Fairfield and Darien, Connecticut, and Scranton, they were all connected to me in that third-floor hospital room. "I'm being put on

a list for two organs—not just a liver, but a heart too. We could be waiting for days or weeks, but the surgery is on."

I turned the floor over to Dr. Fung, who explained the whole situation in medical detail, then discussed how and when to get everyone
here for the operation.

The next morning—Sunday—Bishop Donald Wuerl of the Pittsburgh diocese dropped by. I hadn't expected it. He had come in alone,
although another priest was waiting outside in the hall. We talked for
a moment and I thanked him for the surprise visit. Then he said,
"Governor, I can give you the sacrament of extreme unction, if you
like."

That stopped me cold. In my survival strategy, I had not considered
last rites. "Bishop, that's very generous of you, but we have time. We
have no idea how long it will be."

I knew, of course, that the sacrament of extreme unction was much
more than a soul's preparation for death. The idea goes well beyond
that. It's a sacrament of the sick, a prayer for healing. That, I was more
than willing to accept. But as a practical matter, I knew all these theological nuances would translate into a forty-point banner headline:
GOVERNOR RECEIVES LAST RITES. And I didn't want them hanging
crepe around the capitol just yet.

"I know," said the Bishop. "But I happen to have the oils with me. It's
all I need, and this will be private. Why don't we just do it now, as long
as I'm here?"

Ellen decided the issue, throwing her support to Bishop Wuerl, and
so I was given last rites. There were no headlines.

That night, Dr. Fung came into the room, ca-
sually chatting about the NBA playoff game I was watching on
television. Something was up. Dr. Fung did not strike me as an avid fan
of the game. As he started pacing about the room, I had the feeling he
was giving me a final once-over before springing some news on me.

He left to go across the hall, to the room where Ellen and the boys
were encamped. Matt and Pat were preparing to leave to spend the

night at the Family House, a house for families of transplant patients, when Dr. Fung suggested they stay a moment. Then he picked up Ellen's phone. Ellen noticed how jumpy he was and said, "Nice clogs, John." She was looking down at his surgery clogs, encrusted, she was sure, with blood from many a transplant operation.

"Oh, these are my good-luck clogs," he said, and turned back to the phone. "Tom . . . Do you want to tell them? I'll wait for you."

Within minutes, Dr. Starzl appeared in Ellen's room, asking everyone to come across the hall to my room.

Framed in the doorway of my hospital room with my wife and two sons, Dr. Starzl made his announcement: "We have a donor."

8

Grand Plans

*The overarching memory of the time when our children
were young is of the sheer fun we all had together.*

IT WAS just like Ellen to notice Dr. Fung's clogs and turn her fears
into a dry remark. She's a worrier, but always she has brought that dry
sense of humor into our lives and into every trouble that came our way.
Whenever I'm in danger of taking myself too seriously, I just have to
look over at Ellen, who with a single look can deflate the most pomp-
ous among us. But it works the other way too. When I miss something
important, I look over at her and immediately understand that something serious is up. In so many ways, her instincts are just plain better
than mine. In every situation, good or bad, somehow just looking at her
brings me back to myself.

I think the closest I have ever come to complete devastation was in
December 1978. It was just before Christmas and I was in my law offices
in Scranton. Our family physician, Dr. Robert Gavin, was on the
phone, telling me about the results of Ellen's tests.

"Malignancy." That ugly, horrible word. I sat stunned for the longest
moment. Ellen had a malignancy in her colon and needed immediate

surgery. The things that all of us worry about every day—in that single, searing moment—seemed suddenly like nothing, nothing at all. Everything else paled into insignificance.

Malignancy. I had never had to deal with anything like that before. An overpowering sense of helplessness came over me. A feeling of exhaustion, desolation. The description the doctor gave me of the problem was clinical. And the details of the description burned into my consciousness like the burning lash of a whip on bare back.

Malignancy. I began to pray. *Please God, don't let her die. Don't take her from me now!*

As sure as she is alive today, I am sure Ellen was saved by the Lord's own hand in answer to my prayer.

One weekend at West Point, where we'd gone to see the Holy Cross football team play Army, Ellen had felt a sharp pain. She went to the doctor the following week, and would have put off any follow-up tests because the pain seemed to have subsided. But within a day or two, she just happened to go to a meeting at the school our children were attending. While she was there, she met the doctor's nurse, who said to her: "Ellen, you really should come in tomorrow so we can arrange for those follow-up tests." That woke us up, and so she went in for the tests. After getting the follow-up test results, Ellen underwent surgery to remove the cancerous growth immediately.

Later the surgeons told us that they had caught the cancer just in time. Having the follow-up test was the thing that saved her life. They were convinced, the doctors added, that they'd removed all the cancerous tissue and that Ellen would get better. But, as always in such cases, there were no guarantees. We had to wait.

Ten years later, in 1988—and with no recurrence—Ellen was pronounced cured.

I'll never forget my euphoria following the operation, when the doctors said she would recover. I called Ellen's aunt, Helen Butler, her mother's youngest sister. We always called her "Babe." I wanted to celebrate, to buy something, anything, for Ellen. So Babe and I went downtown and I bought Ellen not one, but two, new coats. And a huge cheesecake. It must have weighed ten pounds. In retrospect, the whole thing seems crazy. But that's what we did. I returned to the house with my offering and laid it before Ellen, who said something like, "Are you out of your mind, Spike?" In a way, I was. I was beside myself with relief and joy. Ellen was okay! She was out of danger! I was a new man. Praise the Lord.

It's amazing to think back on our life and recall how little real planning went into it. We never set out with any grand plans for the future. We just sort of improvised along the way. When we moved into the house on North Washington Avenue in 1962, we didn't say, "Let's live in this house forever!" But that's what we ended up doing. It never seriously occurred to us to move. After the birth of our first child, we didn't say, "Okay, seven more to go." We had no idea how many children we were going to have. No goals, limits, timetables, financial calculations. Before all was said and done, we had eight children in a house with one shower: Margi, Mary Ellen, Kate, Bobby, Chris, Erin, Pat, and Matt. A welcome addition to our household was Ellen's mother, who lived with us into her nineties, with various other relatives coming and going along the way.

From the start, the only real plan Ellen and I followed was that whatever came our way—whatever joys and whatever troubles—we would live them together. "The greatest freedom of all," as G.K. Chesterton wrote, "is the freedom to bind oneself." I don't think I even knew what freedom was until, with Ellen and our children, I found myself bound up inextricably in a life full of promises and obligations.

Our life was simple, but rich in the joys of watching our children grow and mature. I've always said that our children have been better than I had any right to expect.

I can still hear Margi reciting "'Twas the Night Before Christmas" at the age of eighteen months as Ellen and I watched proudly. Somehow "Christmas" came out sounding like "Crippen." And Mary Ellen was the master at assembling a "committee" to help her prepare her exhibit at the science fair. It was always a white-knuckled rush to make the deadline—a good lesson in assigning things to committees. Of all our children, Mary Ellen was the one who had the most friends and busiest social calendar. Constant activity. Perpetual motion. And lots of happy, fun-filled memories of their comings and goings.

Kate was the one who always kept us laughing, with her stories and patented expressions and hilarious gestures. Bobby as a kid was determined to become, in his words as a child, "a carpenter or hunter," aspirations now forgotten as he tracks down voters this year in his campaign to become the next auditor general of Pennsylvania. I recall Chris bumping his face on a picnic bench and losing a front tooth. Chris remembers it a little differently, insisting to this day that Bobby came at him with the bench in "a naked act of aggression." Bobby, if so, got his just desserts soon afterward when he fell in front of our house on North Washington and lost a couple of front teeth. And one of the dividends of my election loss in 1978 was the time it gave me to see Pat play shortstop for his Little League team. Erin, "our littlest daughter," as she used to sign her Christmas cards to Ellen and me, wrote a beautiful essay about summers growing up at Lake Ariel. It brought tears to my eyes.

My kids like to remind me how I embarrassed them at high-school basketball games, yelling at referees about their obvious visual impairments. Matt said he used to beg me to be quiet, even looking to Ellen for help. Bobby delights in telling the story about the time I ducked behind the door to leave him alone with a broom to do battle with a bat in our attic.

As for Ellen's mother, the house would not have been complete without her. It may be hard to believe, but not a day goes by without one of us using one of her favorite expressions, or laughing at something she said when she was with us. She played a large part in our family for years and years. She taught us how to grow old with dignity and good humor. She taught our children how to respect older people. Her life was purposeful and giving to the end.

The morning after I was elected governor, reporters and TV camera people had overrun our house. They were everywhere, taking pictures, interviewing family members. "Nonny," as we called her, was oblivious to all the commotion—that is, until they invaded her domain, the kitchen. Standing at the stove, she ordered them all out of the house because they were interfering with her routine. They all obeyed like sheep, and things quieted down quickly. In retrospect, maybe I should have appointed her to be my press secretary.

I never knew any of my own grandparents. I would like to have known them, but they died before I was born. I did not realize until later that not knowing your grandparents leaves a void in your life. That's why I'm happy that my mother and dad lived to see at least some of the children—and, of course, that Ellen's parents lived to see most of our children.

My father was the first of the grandparents to die, passing away September 6, 1956. But he lived to see Margi. I remember bringing her to see him in his law office. She was probably about a year old, and Ellen had her all dressed up for the visit. When we walked into his office, his eyes lit up and he became more animated than I had ever seen him. He was usually very reserved, but he melted as I handed Margi to him and he held her in his arms.

Margi told me that after my father died, my mother would show her a picture of my father standing next to Margi, who was seated on a horse. "You remember Al, your grandfather, don't you?" my mother would ask. And Margi would say that she did, confiding to me that she didn't really but wanted to please my mother. She had no recollection at all of my father.

My mother lived three years longer than my father, passing away November 9, 1959. When we moved back to Scranton from Washington in 1957, we lived with her for a time in the house on Wyoming Avenue. Then we moved into an apartment on North Webster Avenue nearby. During those years my mother got to know Margi, Mary Ellen, and Kate, who was just an infant when my mother died. They were the joys of her life.

Ellen's dad had a strong influence on our children. He lived to see all of the kids except Matt. And he was at our house almost every day, fixing things, helping Ellen in so many ways. His nickname was "Bomba." He loved the kids. We stayed with Ellen's parents in the summertime at Lake Ariel in Wayne County, about twenty miles from Scranton, so the kids really got to know Bomba well. Swimming. Up on the roof patching up the cottage. Coming home from the store. Taking the kids here and there. I think Bomba spent more time with Bobby than any of the others. When Chris lost a tooth bumping the picnic bench, Bobby's response was, "Bomba will fix it!" When he died in 1967 the kids had to confront death for the first time.

One of my happiest memories as a father is a summer day in 1970. It was not long after I had lost, for the second time, the Democratic primary for governor. I was feeling kind of down, and also guilty that I hadn't been spending as much time as I'd have liked with the children. So I decided to take Bobby and Chris to see the Pirates play. We drove to Pittsburgh in our Ford Country Squire station wagon and stayed at a Howard Johnson's motel in Oakland near the ballpark. A friend of mine from Pittsburgh had arranged for the boys to have some pictures taken by the photographer for the Pittsburgh Pirates. The Pirates were facing the St. Louis Cardinals in one of the last games at old Forbes Field. The Pirates' franchise player at the time was, of course, the incomparable Roberto Clemente.

We went down to the field before the game and my boys met several of the Pirates, including third baseman, Richie Hebner, who spent a few minutes talking with them and having his picture taken. After the Cards had finished their pre-game drills and were walking back to their dressing room, Bobby and Chris walked up to Richie Allen and asked for his autograph. Allen didn't even respond to them—not a word, not a gesture. He just walked right on as if they weren't even there. At Yankee Stadium once, the boys had received a similar brush-off from Boog Powell of the Baltimore Orioles. Maybe both men were having a bad day, but I have never understood how professional athletes could live with themselves after treating admiring kids that way.

My faith in human nature was restored the same day when we met the great Roberto Clemente. He spent all kinds of time with Bobby and Chris. When Clemente died only a year later in the crash of a plane carrying food and medical supplies to the victims of a terrible earthquake in Nicaragua, we grieved for him. We still cherish the pictures taken that day when the great Clemente stopped to give the boys just those few minutes of his time.

I was away a great deal, so most of the daily routine and the discipline fell to Ellen. She showered love and affection on all our children. But she ran a tight ship, and our children knew it. The most telling evidence that she did something right is that in adulthood our children have voted with their feet, coming back for long stays here with their own husbands, wives, and children.

The overarching memory of the time when our children were young is of the sheer fun we all had together. In the summer, when the kids were small, we went to our little cottage at Lake Ariel. We eventually grew out of that little place which had belonged to Ellen's mother and dad, so we reluctantly decided to sell it. When the house came back on the market years later, Margi and her husband, Bill McGrath, bought it and live there now in the summer with their family. After being away from "the lake" for years, Ellen and I bought a big place just two doors down from Margi. We're now their neighbors. And when we drop by, we're usually accompanied by a host of sons, daughters, and grandchildren.

I have never really stopped to formulate a "philosophy" of parenting. Ellen and I simply believed in letting our children find their own way, knowing that we expected them to do their best. Most important of all, we always presented the children with a united front: We treated each other with respect and made our decisions as one. Drawing from my own childhood, I cannot remember ever hearing my own father and mother raising their voices in anger at each other. Ellen and I have always tried to follow that example. The best thing any two parents can do for their children, after all, is to love each other. That's where it all begins.

I had been elected to the State Senate in 1962. During that time I practiced law by myself part-time in between Senate duties. Then in 1964 I joined with two friends, Jim Haggerty and Frank McDonnell, to form our own law firm. You guessed it: Casey, Haggerty & McDonnell. We stayed together until 1969 when I was elected auditor general. Jim and Frank remained strong supporters through all my political ups and downs. When I was elected governor, they were still law partners, and I appointed Jim to the cabinet as secretary of the commonwealth and later counsel to the governor. He took on a lot of tough jobs and performed them with skill and dedication. Frank served faithfully as treasurer of the Democratic State Committee. Both remain close friends to this day.

My first cause as a state senator was helping children. Shortly after taking office, I heard about a problem known at the time as PKU. It was an acronym for the long, clinical name of a birth defect which prevented an infant from metabolizing certain foods, including milk. Undetected, the ingestion of such food would cause normal babies to become mentally retarded. For some reason the state of Pennsylvania had no law on its books requiring the simple test needed to detect the presence of PKU. Once detected, a simple change in diet could correct the problem. Babies throughout Pennsylvania who might have been spared were instead being born with that defect going undetected.

The test cost practically nothing, I learned. So why weren't we requiring it by law? It did not strike me as a complex problem. So we passed a simple law—just a few lines on paper—requiring that Pennsylvania's babies be given the PKU test. Thirty years later I still count it as among the best things I ever did. A simple change in diet can protect a child from a lifetime of retardation, thanks to the passage of that simple law. I remember reading a small article a few months afterward about the first baby who had been found in Pennsylvania with PKU since the new law had taken effect. A healthy, beautiful baby, saved from mental retardation.

The story, however, makes it sound as if Pennsylvania politics was a lofty business in which I was always weighing pressing moral questions. Anyone familiar with our state at the time, or with practical politics in general, would have a good laugh at that suggestion.

My initiation into statewide politics began at age thirty-four when, restless in the state Senate, I first set my sights on the governor's seat.

Service in the Senate was a frustrating experience. I was in the minority party, and, well, I was thirty-four, knew everything, and felt just sure I was ready to run the whole show. I marvel at my audacity at the time. But some young men are like that, and I was the most self-assured of the type.

The first stop was in the office of David L. Lawrence. He had been mayor of Pittsburgh and governor of Pennsylvania. His political maxims included such gems as: "Never write a letter—and never throw one away." And: "Never *write* what you can *say*. And never *say* what you can *wink*. . . ."

When I met with Governor Lawrence in Pittsburgh, accompanied by Lackawanna County Democratic Chairman Patrick Mellody, he put matters very simply: "Your candidacy makes no sense. You're too young. You're not identified with any statewide issue and, besides, you're Catholic."

Governor Lawrence was a Catholic himself, but still wary of the electoral prospects of Catholic candidates in Pennsylvania. He had initially opposed John F. Kennedy's candidacy for president, in part because Kennedy was Catholic.

I was not about to see my career sidetracked by a wink from Lawrence, and said so to Mellody as we left that day. "Who does he think he is, telling me I can't run for governor!" I announced my candidacy several days later.

Despite Lawrence's misgivings, I got the endorsement of the Democratic State Committee, but was immediately opposed for the Democratic nomination by a millionaire businessman named Milton Shapp. Shapp had made a fortune in the cable television business and had been part of several highly publicized public causes that had gained him name recognition across the state.

Until then, in Pennsylvania and elsewhere, the endorsement of the party had been enough to ensure nomination in the primary. No endorsed candidate ever spent much money in a Democratic gubernatorial primary, because by then it was pretty much a done deal.

Shapp changed that. He spent $1.4 million of his own money on his primary campaign. It was the most lavishly financed campaign in Pennsylvania history. He hired the best experts in the country and flooded radio and television and the mail with his message. His most innovative tactic was a feature-length film about himself. It was the story of the American dream: A Horatio Alger saga about this man who started on a coal truck in Cleveland and went on to become a millionaire in the new hi-tech world of cable television.

To create it, he hired one of the best filmmakers in the country, a man named Guggenheim. Shapp paid him seventy-five thousand dollars—in those days, an unheard of sum for such a thing. The documentary ran hundreds of times across the state. The film was entertaining, with powerful visual effects. It was called *The Man Against the Machine.*

Of course, in this drama, Shapp was the man and I was the machine. This was ludicrous because Shapp had, in effect, bought "the machine" and greased it with more money than it had ever had. But the film could not have been more effective. It was the first use of massive spending and massive media, created and executed by experts.

Unwisely, I chose not to answer his attacks. His lavish spending, aided by my inept campaign effort, helped him eke out a narrow fifty-thousand-vote victory from the million votes cast. The Shapp campaign brought to Pennsylvania the new world of big money, big media, and big campaign-consultant politics.

As it turned out, Shapp's spending won him the primary but lost him the election. The big money came back to haunt him. His Republican opponent in the November election, Lieutenant Governor Raymond Shafer, filed a legal challenge under the election law to Shapp's spending reports. Court hearings dragged on for weeks and the results were damaging to the Shapp campaign. In November, Shapp lost.

That first loss in the primary was a blow, but soon other things came along and I put it behind me. In 1967, I was elected as a delegate to a statewide convention to rewrite the state constitution. For three months, the work was a full-time job. At the urging of Jack Lynch, who had helped manage my campaign against Shapp, and Walter Giesey, former chief of staff to Governor Lawrence, I decided to run for another statewide office, auditor general. The auditor general was Pennsylvania's chief fiscal officer.

And so I became a statewide candidate again in 1968. This was the year of the Democratic Party's Convention in Chicago, so marked with rancor and confrontation over the war in Vietnam.

I attended the convention and was appalled by the sorry treatment of our nominee, Hubert Humphrey. That year I came to know and respect Humphrey greatly. It was Humphrey who spoke of the Democratic Party's basic mission: To help "those in the dawn of life, those in the shadows of life, and those in the twilight of life."

His words summed up for me what it meant to call myself a Democrat. Whatever its faults, at the end of the day, to be a Democrat was to have a mission. To be a Democrat was to identify with the afflicted, the vulnerable, the powerless. Let the other party look after those at the plateaus and summits of life. Democrats would look to those still struggling down below. That was the Democratic Party of my father, and Humphrey spoke for it. In some ways he was the last party leader to do so. Those protesters in Chicago who would go on to oppose so vehemently Richard Nixon had themselves, in part, to thank for Nixon's election. They treated our nominee disgracefully, with the nation watching.

Hubert Humphrey was also very generous to the lesser lights on the ticket—people like me. He spent a great deal of time in his speeches calling attention to the statewide candidates and making their election an integral part of his message. I remember campaigning together with him on a flat-bed trailer at the gate of the huge Westinghouse plant in East Pittsburgh, after Chubby Checker had warmed up the crowd for us. I was very grateful and proud to be on the party ticket with Humphrey. I also admired his strong sense of loyalty to President Johnson under the most difficult of circumstances. I have always placed a high premium on loyalty in politics—loyalty to those who have helped, to those with whom you have served, and to those with whom you have made common cause.

I won the election in 1968 by over four hundred thousand votes and threw everything I had into the office.

On paper, the auditor general has no real power. If you read the statutes, you'd find them dry as dust. They just say, in effect, "The auditor general shall audit." But I took the aggressive approach, using that power to the fullest.

For instance, Pennsylvania has 501 school districts, so we had to audit all 501—including reviewing all the receipts and expense accounts that all 501 generated. When the directors of the districts would go to a convention, each would submit bills for reimbursement for their motel rooms. So I would send a staff member to check the room numbers of the motel. Sometimes we'd find out that there was no "room twenty-nine" in the Big Springs Motel that Director X supposedly had occupied. Was this a mistake, or was somebody trying to pull a fast one at the taxpayer's expense? We would find out and hold the guilty party accountable.

A story I used to tell our staff involved a man who defrauded some of the biggest banks in the country. He was in the salad oil business and kept borrowing big money, using the salad oil as collateral. The banks were lining up to give him money. After all, he had huge tanks in which to store all that salad oil! No one at any of the banks, however, had thought about checking to see if there was actually any oil in the tanks. There wasn't. The incident gave rise to a saying we used around the office: "Be sure to look in the tank."

During my early days as auditor general, my chief deputy was Jack Lynch. He was surprised to see the various bureau directors walk into our offices carrying hefty sums of money, all in cash and checks. The money had just been collected from the employees on payday as political "contributions" to the Democratic State Committee. Jack knew, of course, that the law required that all political contributions be strictly *voluntary*, not collected as a matter of course on payday—when the fear of losing one's job was enough for all to pitch in. Amazed, Jack called me immediately.

"Tell the bureau directors to return the money to the employees immediately," I told him. "Tell them also to stop the practice—and never repeat it." For emphasis, I also added that anyone engaging in that kind of practice would be fired on the spot.

Not long after that, various Democratic county chairmen took to stopping by. The employees in my office were political appointees; these chairmen would come to us when they were having a political dinner or some such fund-raiser. "What is your policy on political contributions by employees?" they would ask.

"You want to know our policy?" I would reply. "Jack, give them the policy." Jack would hand them a copy of the state law. "Read the statute," I'd say. "When you read the statute, you have read the policy. That *is* the policy. We follow the law."

I remember one chairman asking with a disturbing chuckle, "Well, we know that's your *official* position, but what's your *real* position?"

"Let me say it to you again. You must have missed it the first time around," I replied. "Read the statute: that is our policy. When you read the statute, you have read the policy. That's it. Period."

I have only one regret about my time as auditor general. I should have been content with the post and not run for governor again in 1970. This was a big mistake. After just two years in the job, it was not the right thing to do.

Once again my opponent was Milton Shapp, lone fighter against the Casey "machine." My campaign was rife with mistakes, including a loss of temper. It involved James H. J. Tate, the mayor of Philadelphia.

If you were a Democrat and wanted to run for anything back then, the man to see was Mayor Tate. He was what we called a "throwback." He ruled with an iron hand. All the time he was mayor, he stayed on as the Democratic leader of the Forty-third Ward in Philadelphia, untroubled by what political philosophers might call the "tension" between those two roles.

So I made the obligatory pilgrimage to his office, and the conversation went like this:

"What county in Ireland did your people come from?"

"From—"

"How do you stand with your Bishop?"

And so on, until I felt like I was in the confessional instead of sitting there with the state's most powerful political leader. The mayor would, in time, become a supporter—at least, for a while. But he confused political support with personal dominance. One day a reporter asked Tate if he was supporting me. "I am supporting Casey," came the reply, "as long as he behaves himself."

Immediately, the reporters tracked me down and asked for my comment. I was furious. "If I win this election," I said, "*I'm* going to be the governor of Pennsylvania and nobody else. If Mayor Tate has any different view, he'd better rethink his position."

That was the end of my Tate support. Within days he announced that he no longer supported me, and with that went an exodus of his supporters to Shapp. Shapp beat me in the primary again, and went on to win the general election to become governor.

Losing was probably a good thing in one respect. I returned to my auditor general job, and was re-elected in 1972. That year I really dodged a political bullet. It was Nixon versus McGovern for President. Nixon carried Pennsylvania by almost a million votes. No one running for a statewide office in Pennsylvania had ever survived a million-vote landslide for the presidential candidate of the other party. I bucked this tide for the first time, winning by a five-hundred-thousand-vote margin.

And then an extraordinary thing happened. The year was 1974. I was approached to run for governor a third time— as a Republican. Shapp had served one term, and under a new law was now allowed to succeed himself. That sealed the Democratic nomination. My differences with Shapp were, of course, well-known in both parties. So Republican leaders thought I might want to switch parties and take him on in his re-election bid in 1974. Delivering this overture to me was ex-Governor William W. Scranton, one of the famous Scranton family my hometown was named after. One Sunday morning in 1974, I was invited to meet with him. When he offered this unusual proposal, I was not in the least bit tempted.

"I appreciate the gesture, Governor," I said, "but all the Caseys have always been Democrats." And that was that. Little did either of us know at the time that just twelve years later, Governor Scranton's son and I would be locked in a no-holds-barred struggle to become governor.

In the last twenty years, many Democrats across America have made a different decision. Their exodus is the central electoral fact of American politics today. It's been a boon to the Republican Party—in the south especially. And it remains a problem for Democratic leaders who are trying in vain to stem the tide.

Those are matters I'll get to later. As for me, my place is in the Democratic Party. Always will be. I would never leave it.

I say this despite what followed after that decision in 1974—a bewildering, chaotic Democratic primary election. A *Philadelphia Inquirer* feature by William Ecenbarger, entitled "The Real Bob Casey," described what happened as "one of the most incredible chapters in the incredible history of American politics." It sure was.

The story begins with Johnny Durbin, a Harrisburg hotel owner with a strong interest in politics. The bar in his hotel, the Senate Hotel, was adorned with the pictures of elected and appointed officials in state government. Many members of the legislature from both parties were regulars at his bar. Johnny knew everybody who was anybody in Pennsylvania politics.

He knew local elected officials too. One of them was Robert E. Casey, Register of Wills in Cambria County, in the Johnstown area. Bob Casey, the register of wills, was a really nice guy. Everybody liked him. He came to Harrisburg often for meetings and conventions. He would stop in to see me in the auditor general's office. His son-in-law was an auditor who worked for my agency.

The traditional next step for a two-term auditor general was to run for state treasurer. When I announced that I would not be a candidate for that post, the story in political circles was that Johnny Durbin convinced Robert E. Casey, the register of wills, to run for state treasurer. He had never run for statewide office before.

The Durbin strategy was simple: File the nomination papers, then lie low. No campaigning. No fundraising. No advertising.

As the story goes, Casey placed only one newspaper ad. It was a small ad on the sports page of *The Pittsburgh Press* on the weekend before the election. The ad said, "Vote for Bob Casey for State Treasurer!" When the person placing the ad was asked whether the ad would contain a picture of the candidate, the paper was informed: No picture.

Casey was nominated with over 40 percent of the vote in a five-candidate Democratic primary. He went on to win the general election handily. His biggest victory margin was in Lackawanna County, my home county. And so he became the state treasurer of Pennsylvania. Robert E. Casey took the oath of office in November 1976. Two months later, in January 1977, my second term as auditor general ended and I became a private citizen again.

Soon after leaving office, I began to think seriously about giving the governorship one more try in 1978. After all, Shapp would be finishing his second term as governor. There would be an open seat for governor. This didn't happen too often, so opportunity had obviously beckoned. I decided to give it another go. As always, the obstacles were formidable.

Pennsylvania is a large, diverse state. The population centers are in the Philadelphia region in the southeast, and the Pittsburgh region in the southwest. A candidate like me, who lives in the less heavily populated northeastern section of the state, is at an immediate disadvantage when running against a candidate from the densely populated Philadelphia or Pittsburgh regions.

I had a serious problem in 1978. My opponents were the popular former mayor of Pittsburgh, Pete Flaherty, and Ernie Kline, the Democratic lieutenant governor who hailed from Beaver Falls, near Pittsburgh. Historically, in the heavily Democratic Pittsburgh area, voters turned out in greater numbers in primary elections than they did in the Philadelphia region of the east. And they tended to vote for western Pennsylvania candidates.

I decided to push ahead anyway. Suddenly, from out of nowhere, another Robert Casey appeared—entering the Democratic primary for lieutenant governor. His name was Robert P. Casey. A Pittsburgh biology teacher who also ran a Baskin-Robbins ice cream store, he had never before run for statewide office. The whole thing sounded familiar.

Then another: One Robert J. Casey from the Pittsburgh area threw his hat into the race for Congress that year.

There were now two Bob Caseys left for the voters to sort out: One candidate for lieutenant governor, and me. Voters in Allegheny County, the second-largest county in the state, would look down to find three Robert Caseys on the ballot; in the other sixty-six counties, there would be two Robert P. Caseys.

My campaign committee filed a lawsuit to have the ballot clearly distinguish between the two names. We suggested that occupations be listed by each candidate's name on the ballot. The court refused to order any change on the ballot.

So I was forced to stand back and watch the inevitable. All I could do was continue to campaign, trying to explain the difference between me and two impostors trading on my name. It was an impossible situation.

Adopting the tried-and-true Durbin strategy, the Pittsburgh Robert P. Casey running for lieutenant governor didn't campaign. He ran a "front porch" campaign, spending a grand total of four thousand dollars. He didn't even put an ad in the paper, with or without a photo. He just sat back and waited. Meanwhile, I raised hundreds of thousands of dollars, advertised extensively on television, and campaigned around the clock.

I lost. The other Robert P. Casey won the Democratic nomination for Lieutenant Governor in a fourteen-candidate field while I lost the same day in the race for governor. Crafty opponents confused the voters even more by telling them they could vote for Flaherty for governor and me for lieutenant governor.

In political circles it all became one big joke. Former Philadelphia Mayor Frank Rizzo called the whole episode "unbelievable," suggesting I change my name to Frank Rizzo.

But I felt miserable. I can't express how frustrated I felt. This was my third try, the one that I had to win. To lose was bad enough—but to lose this way! It was just what had happened to my dad years earlier in his bid for office. It was humiliating.

Of course, poor Flaherty, the Democratic gubernatorial nominee, was left with problems of his own. His running mate was an impostor who had never held public office. The Republican candidate, U.S.

Attorney Richard Thornburgh, was on the attack. Flaherty was forced, in effect, to say publicly and loudly, "I'm not running with him. I don't even know the guy."

It was wild. Thornburgh won the governorship and Flaherty went down to defeat with the other Robert P. Casey. In November, that other Casey lost to William W. Scranton III.

The election loss was a bitter pill for me to swallow. I had worked hard for fifteen long years in big-state politics, trying to make my name stand for something good in the eyes of the people. And suddenly it seemed that all the fruits of that labor were taken from me. The hurt was like an open wound for a long time afterward. Ultimately, it gave me the drive to try once more to grab for the brass ring and run for governor. As one commentator put it: "Casey's name is magic for everyone but him."

I made up my mind right then and there that those words would not become my political epitaph.

9

Tomorrow

Now the enormity of what I was facing seemed to close in on me. I felt myself becoming apprehensive, uneasy. The better term is just plain scared.

IN MY hospital room, there was a "big game" atmosphere. The operation was set for five o'clock the next morning. The room was the scene of frenzied activity: Troopers standing sentry outside the door. The transfer of power over to Lieutenant Governor Mark Singel. Doctors and nurses coming and going. Ellen and me planning how to get our children there in time.

The family communications network was put into high gear. Pat called Mary Ellen and Margi, both living in Connecticut, saying, "They found a donor. You have to get out here as soon as you can!"

That started a mad dash through the night for all eight of the Casey children. By car, by plane, one after another, they dropped everything to get to Pittsburgh before the operation began—Margi, Mary Ellen, Kate, Erin, Bobby, to join Pat and Matt, who were already there. By the time we received news of the donor, it was nearing midnight.

We quickly chartered two planes to meet some of the children in Scranton since Erin, Bobby, and Kate lived there. Margi and Mary

Ellen drove frantically from Connecticut to Scranton to meet the planes. Bobby and his wife, Terese, Erin, Kate, and Pat Boles (who worked in my office) were on the first plane, arriving at the hospital around 2:00 A.M. Margi and Mary Ellen took the second plane, which landed in Pittsburgh at about 3:00 A.M.

We had difficulty finding Chris, who was somewhere en route back to Washington, D.C., from a class reunion at Holy Cross College in Massachusetts. Pat had left several messages on his answering machine. Chris finally called Pat after arriving in Washington, minutes after the donor was found.

There were no flights to Pittsburgh that late, so Chris rented a car and made the five-hour trip to the hospital in a record three-and-a-half, accelerating with each report he heard on CNN radio, announcing that I was dying.

Somehow they all made it by about 3:45 A.M. when around me stood my eight children. At first we didn't talk about the things you would expect a family to talk about at a time like that. Nothing heavy; just the opposite.

We just talked about the things we always talked about. Matt, Pat, and I, for instance, were convulsed with laughter as we recounted for the perhaps fiftieth time an episode from our favorite old television series, *The Honeymooners*, starring Jackie Gleason and Art Carney. No matter how many times I'd seen each episode of that old program, it broke me up—every time. And the two of them knew it. Even then, I thought how incongruous this must seem to a non-family onlooker. Chris, expecting a somber scene, walked in just as we got to the part in one episode where Gleason makes one of those bug-eyed faces we always found so hilarious, and I was broken up with laughter. We found ourselves doing that night what we had done so often together over the years. And it was a tonic for me. It was wonderful.

Ellen and the children would come into my room, we would talk, then they would leave, moving back and forth between Ellen's room across the hall and mine. I would close my eyes for a few minutes to rest them, only for a brief time. I was exhausted, but at a moment like that the last thing on your mind is a cat-nap.

Then the moment arrived. The surgeons were ready. One by one, almost in birth order, the kids came in to see me.

With each one, I had a special moment, telling each how proud and happy they'd always made me. There were hugs and kisses and "I love you's" as I repeated over and over, "Don't worry, I'm going to make it. Make it just fine."

Margi, the eldest, and the one who never falls apart, had said to everyone before it began, "Whatever you do, try your hardest not to cry." But then her turn came, and when I began, "Margi, you were our first. . . ." she dissolved into tears.

To Pat, Matt, Mary Ellen, Chris, and Bobby, I told them what good sons and daughters they'd been, what strong characters they had, how they were never to sell themselves short, never forget where they came from, never give up their goals.

Each one, each different, eight in a row, down to our "littlest daughter" Erin, now a mother herself. I wanted all of them to know how much I loved them. How proud I was of each one of them. What a joy they had been for Ellen and me.

And then there was Kate, defiant and determined, saying, "Fight, Dad! Fight like you've never fought before!"

"I will, Kate," I said. "I will. Don't worry."

Finally, Ellen came into the room. We are private people, even in front of our children. And the prior eight years had brought few truly private moments. The children rarely witnessed shows of emotion from either of us, but that night things were different; all formality fell away, and they saw their invincible mother crying.

"You can't leave me yet," Ellen was saying to me.

"I'm not going anywhere," I said, holding her hand to never let go, "I promise." It was hard for me to see her that way too. I don't think I ever had before, and I would have done anything to dry her tears. "I'll see you tomorrow," was all I could say, again and again. "I'll see you tomorrow. I promise you."

There, in that dimly-lit hospital room, we went through our long life together.

Before the nurses came in, one of my state troopers—State Police

Sergeant John Kulick—gave me a prayer to read. It was a prayer to St. Joseph that he'd carried with him into battle in Vietnam, a prayer for safety and deliverance. I read every word. Later, after Ellen had watched me disappear behind the operating room doors, Trooper Michael Donley, who had also fought in Vietnam, handed Ellen the same prayer.

The nurses placed me on a gurney and wheeled me into the hall where all the children were waiting. They all surrounded the gurney and followed me down the corridor to the elevator, and I saw, like snapshots, a face here, a smile there, a rush of bodies keeping up.

The attendants moved me into the elevator. With Ellen holding my hand and troopers by my side, I looked back at all my grown children's faces bunched together in the hallway, framed by the elevator doors. They were all smiling and waving and calling out encouraging words. At a loss for words as the elevator closed, I gave them a thumbs up sign. My last sight of them was their heads pressed together, straining for one last glimpse of me.

We moved several floors down to the hall leading to the operating suite. As the doors swung open to the operating room, Ellen and I had time for one more good-bye before we parted. We embraced and said, just one more time, how much we loved each other.

From the time I first saw Ellen Harding when we were both fourteen, she has always been the most beautiful woman in the world. Strikingly, softly beautiful. Her beauty is rivaled only by her goodness. For forty-three years I have rejoiced in her graces. She has lived, not for herself, but for me and for our children. She has spent her entire life giving—giving to all of us and to all who needed her. Her generosity is spontaneous and self-starting; it comes from within. It requires no prodding. It's a gift beyond anything I could ever deserve. I marvel at her goodness, but also at her gentleness and strength.

She is silk. She is velvet. She is burnished gold. But she is also steel. I thank God for her every day. Since my surgery, I have come to love her and to depend upon her more than ever. She has made my life a joy. How blessed I have been to spend my life with her!

I was determined to keep my promise to her. I looked forward, as never before, to "seeing her tomorrow," as I began the fight of my life.

As the gurney came to rest, a group of doctors appeared around me. They were the anesthesiologists who would put me to sleep. Now the enormity of what I was facing seemed to close in on me. I felt myself becoming apprehensive, uneasy. The better term is just plain scared.

Just then one of the doctors, a young woman who was attending near the gurney, looked down at me. She put her hand on my forearm, as if to say, "Don't worry, everything is going to be all right." It transformed me. Just that little reassuring touch, one human being touching another, gave me calm, brought me back to myself. As suddenly as I had felt the rush of panic, I was again at peace. I was ready. The last thing I remember was that touch.

10

Riding the Horse

". . . for a hundred years they told us that shoveling the manure was as good as riding the horse."

"Well," he went on, "in 1986, when Casey ran, we decided to ride the horse."

"CASEY'S NAME is magic for everyone but him." That political postscript stuck like a bone in my throat. The bizarre outcome of the election of 1978 really got to me. It just seemed so terribly unfair. I was not going to leave it at that.

A comeback, however, would have to wait eight years, and when it came it would be harder than ever—like pushing a large rock up a steep hill.

"Ellen," I said one morning in 1985, "I'm thinking about running for governor one last time." In the time since the election of 1978, I had joined the Philadelphia law firm of Dilworth, Paxson, Kalish & Kauffman and was doing well at it. It was only seven months after the '78 primary election that we learned of Ellen's cancer, and that experience had brought us even closer together. Our children were going their way, the eldest now thirty-one, the youngest fourteen. In general, we had left state politics to others and were heeding the philosopher's advice to tend our own garden.

But even before that, when I was auditor general, I don't think I had ever made politics the center of my life anyway. During campaigns, maybe. But campaigns are like that. They're sprints. You hold your life in suspension, put your head down, and run. And when it's over you try to get your life back to normal. That's what we were during that period—a normal family. I did not spend those seven years morosely replaying the events of 1978. When I did stop to think about it, it bothered me. But I did not regard this period as my "wilderness years" or anything so melodramatic—all the while plotting my political comeback. If you caught me on most days, I'd have been thinking and talking about the routine things of life like paying tuition bills, beating the traffic, or raking the leaves.

I did read the newspapers, however, out of more than just curiosity or civic-mindedness. As 1985 rolled around, I suddenly began to see the political planets coming into alignment over Scranton. Governor Richard Thornburgh was finishing his second term. His heir apparent was Lieutenant Governor William W. Scranton III. It was just taken for granted in political circles that Scranton, scion of the Scranton family, son of the former governor, would become the next governor. There was an air of inevitability about it all. I'd made more than my share of mistakes in politics, but I knew one thing for sure: Whenever the pundits declare someone's election "inevitable"—read "vulnerable." When the heir apparent himself starts believing in his invincibility, it's time for a reality check.

Beyond that, I just had a feeling about 1986. I just felt it was our moment, and said so to Ellen when I first put the idea to her that afternoon.

"If you want to do it, it's okay with me," she answered. "But are you prepared to lose, Spike?" she asked.

"Ellen," I answered, "are you prepared to *win?*"

To be honest, though, even after that confident reply, I was the one who wavered. Did I *really* want to go through it again? I wasn't sure.

So I kicked the idea around a few weeks more, until one weekend I found myself back at Holy Cross to visit my son Pat. I had thought long and hard about running during the four-hour trip from Scranton to Worcester.

"What about it, Dad? Are you going to run again?" Pat asked.

"I don't think so," I said. Actually I wasn't really sure, but somehow that's the answer that came out. I think I was just a little weary at the whole prospect of doing it all over again. And I'd begun to think through the logistics: I had no campaign staff in waiting. No financiers eager to bankroll my fourth run for governor. No pundits calling on me to return to politics for the good of the state. For all practical purposes, I had nobody and nothing. I would be starting from scratch. And Dick Caliguiri, the popular mayor of Pittsburgh, and Ed Rendell, the strongest vote-getter in Philadelphia, were actively considering a run.

"Well, why don't you think about it some more, Dad," suggested Pat. "If you don't, we'll always wonder what might have been. I say—do it! And this time, we'll be there with you. This time, let's run like we've never run before."

Without a great deal more agonizing, I decided to do it. Before long we had our campaign going. We called our campaign committee "The Real Bob Casey Committee." Our unofficial slogan was: "It's my name, and I'm back to claim it." I announced my candidacy in Pittsburgh in January 1986, promising, if elected, to go to Monessen to dramatize my resolve to help struggling people there and all across the state.

But Pat was right: this time we were going to do things differently. During my eight years on the sidelines, things had changed. What Shapp had pioneered in 1966 was now the norm: mass-media politics, lots of money, experts, full-time pollsters, professional consultants—in short, the modern political campaign.

The man to start with in '86, I decided, was Pat Caddell. He'd been Jimmy Carter's pollster and was now the Democratic Party's premier political pollster. Based in Washington, he was now consulting for big-league candidates and major corporations around the country. Apart from Caddell's expertise, I figured that having him on board would alert the Pennsylvania press and political establishment to the seriousness of my intentions. It would make it harder for them to write me off from the start, as some seemed so eager to do.

Caddell's associate, Paul Maslin, was due to come through Philadelphia on other business, and agreed to meet me. I gave Maslin all the reasons why I thought I could win. Then I got to my main point. "Paul," I said, "thanks for coming. I appreciate your being here. But I want to talk to Pat Caddell."

"Pat's very busy," he told me. "He's working with Coca-Cola on the 'New Coke' account."

"Well," I said. "I know he's busy, but I have to see him."

Finally Maslin agreed. Arrangements were made for me to meet the great man in Washington.

My son Bobby had told me that Caddell had just teamed up with top Democratic political consultants David Doak and Bob Shrum. The brand-new firm was the hottest Democratic political consulting group in the country. If I could land them for my campaign, friend and foe alike would know I meant business. What's more, as I learned later, one of Caddell's clients was Mayor Dick Caliguiri.

On the appointed day, four of my children in tow, I arrived at the Washington offices of Caddell, Doak, & Shrum. Bob Shrum was a gifted speechwriter and media consultant. David Doak was a talented and seasoned manager who had just helped elect Mark White governor of Texas.

What I most remember about that first meeting was the oppressive heat in their finely appointed office suites. It was a sweltering Washington day but for some reason there was no air conditioning, as if they were still observing the energy conservation program of the Carter era. Caddell came in wearing a Harris tweed sport coat, sweating as if he'd just done a few laps around the Mall, but he never took off that jacket. He walked to his desk and sat down behind a huge pile of papers. I launched into my presentation. Around the room were Doak and Shrum; my children Margi, Kate, Bobby, and Chris; and John Elliott, a Philadelphia lawyer and one of the prime movers of my campaign in those early days.

I figured they would give me short shrift. I knew I had to talk fast and get right to the point. I can't remember how I opened my remarks, but I remember being very intense and emotional about my ability to win.

From behind his mound of papers, Caddell didn't seemed very stirred by my appeal. He kept leaving and then re-entering the room. I had the feeling his mind was on the "New Coke" account. His seeming detachment bugged me.

Suddenly I cut through all the political analysis, discarded my re-hearsed arguments, and spoke from the heart.

"Look," I said, "I'm a member of a big law firm in Philadelphia. I'm doing pretty well for myself. A few months ago, I was at the Bellevue Stratford Hotel in Philadelphia. I was in my room surrounded by law books and briefs and papers. I was preparing two cases for argument before the Third Circuit Court of Appeals. I was working morning, noon, and night. It was January and freezing outside.

"On Sunday morning, I left the hotel to go to church, and outside on one of the sidewalk grates, I saw something. It was this lump under an old rug covered with snow and ice. Steam was coming up all around it. It was cold—I mean, like ten degrees cold. When I walked a little further, I saw it was a man. And I just stood and looked at him.

"You know what I did then? What we all do. I went about my business. I went to church and then back to the Bellevue. But the image of that man on the grate stuck in my mind. Why do I want to be governor of Pennsylvania? Well, let's start with that guy. We need to help him, a fellow human being wrapped in a rug on a freezing street in our biggest city. And that was the beginning for me—the beginning of the process that, after three campaigns, led me to decide to try again: To leave the law and try to make a difference for all those people out there who are hurting, and who need help."

And I meant every word of it. It got Caddell's attention. For the first time, he looked up from his papers straight at me, and said: "You ought to go to Pittsburgh tomorrow, get a megaphone, and shout that from a street corner!"

The meeting went on for two hours, turning back to the practicalities of actually winning the primary election just months away. Soon Caddell, Doak, and Shrum had signed on to handle my campaign. They would do the polling and the TV commercials. Just as I'd hoped, word got out and suddenly my stock was rising.

The next slot to fill was campaign manager. "Any ideas?" I asked Doak one day.

"Well," he said, "there's this guy. . . . Hasn't won yet. But he's tough, a fighter. Good with the press. He's focused. And he protects his candidate. I think he's the best there is."

I asked what his name was.

"James Carville. He's from Louisiana but he's in Austin, Texas, now. And he has a young sidekick named Paul Begala."

I asked Doak if he would call Carville and ask him if he would meet me at our campaign headquarters in Philadelphia.

So one Sunday morning, down the steps of our basement campaign headquarters came James Carville. As he came inside, suit bag slung over his shoulder, I noticed the eyes. He reminded me of the gunfighter in the classic Western from the fifties, *Shane*. Remember the young Jack Palance, the hired gunfighter brought in to take care of Alan Ladd? Those deep-set eyes? That was my first thought on meeting James Carville. Same eyes. The eyes of a gunfighter.

We would be in for some tough going. *This guy looks like he can handle it*, I thought.

"I don't make any big claims," Carville began, looking around. "What's wrong now may still be wrong after I come in here. What you have to do is very simple. You have to raise money. And then more money. And you have to develop your message and stick with it. . . ."

Carville's a piece of work. I'd known some characters but never anybody quite like him. Little by little it dawned on me that I liked Carville. For all our differences, we had at least one thing in common. He'd lost enough to really, really want this one. Politically, we were both looking into the same abyss. He was hungry, ready to scratch and claw his way to victory, whatever the odds. Carville worked around the clock. And he drove everyone else in the campaign to work at the same frenzied pace.

Caddell, Doak, and Shrum decided that our campaign theme would take what some considered a major weakness—three prior primary losses—and turn it into an asset. So they came up with the slogan, "Bob Casey is coming back, and so is Pennsylvania." This was the tagline on the TV spots, and we repeated the theme over and over in all of our advertising. It caught on. It gave our whole effort a positive, confident thrust.

With Carville's arrival, everything was ready. I hit the road and the phone—hard. Even with the best advisers, I was the longest of long shots. Over the previous twenty-five years, I'd been on almost every road in Pennsylvania. Now I had to do it all over again. I started in the southwest, the heart of the state's Democratic strength. I collared and persuaded potential allies wherever I could find them. Slowly the effort began to pay off. My first big breakthrough was the support of Allegheny County Commissioner Tom Foerster.

And our first big group endorsement came in a meeting in New Stanton, Pennsylvania, of Democratic commissioners from key counties in the southwest. The group passed a resolution of support for my candidacy. After thanking them, I walked straight to the nearest pay phone and called the *Pittsburgh Post Gazette* to announce that I had "the support of a broad group of influential county commissioners in some of the most Democratic counties of the state."

Then I got a real break. Mayor Caliguiri decided not to run for governor. This boost enabled me to consolidate my support in Allegheny County, the state's second-largest county after Philadelphia. Later in the primary season County Commissioner Pete Flaherty (who had beaten me in the 1978 primary) endorsed me; his declaration helped a great deal. Caliguiri, Flaherty, and Foerster all appeared in TV commercials endorsing my candidacy. We ran those ads in the heavily Democratic Pittsburgh television market.

Meanwhile, the man to beat for the Democratic nomination was Philadelphia district attorney Ed Rendell. The word in political circles was he'd gained then-Mayor Wilson Goode's support with assurances that he would not challenge Goode for mayor. Early on, Goode made it clear he was not a supporter of mine, which discouraged the city's other officials from backing me. In time, though, some came over, including City Councilman John White. I also won the support of the Democratic State Committee after a raucous meeting in Harrisburg. Rendell denounced the vote, with echoes of Shapp's "man-against-machine" theme twenty years earlier. This was the time-honored practice in Pennsylvania politics: Try your best to round up the support of the Democratic organization. If you fail, then turn around and bravely denounce "the machine."

In February 1986, the time came to pick a running mate. In Pennsylvania primary elections, the governor and lieutenant governor are chosen separately; the winners in each race then run together as a ticket in the general election. It was important that someone I would be compatible with be nominated for lieutenant governor.

Carville and most of my advisers wanted me to choose a state representative from Washington County named David Sweet, a man with a good record from a strong Democratic county. Most of the Democratic politicians in the western counties feared that Pittsburgh City Controller Tom Flaherty would win the nomination for lieutenant governor because people would think he was Pete Flaherty, the popular former mayor. In Allegheny County, meanwhile, Commissioner Tom Foerster was pushing hard for County Controller Frank Lucchino to be my running mate.

After thinking long and hard about this key decision, I made up my mind. I was determined to pick a running mate who was pro-life. In early March, I decided on State Senator Mark Singel from Cambria County, who had a consistent pro-life record. He was very popular in Cambria County, the Johnstown area, a strong Democratic region.

With that, all hell broke loose. I had an open revolt on my hands. The Allegheny County leaders, still smarting because I chose Singel instead of Lucchino, were convinced that Tom Flaherty would surely beat Singel. Whatever chance I had of winning the general election, they were convinced, was lost with the selection of Singel.

Later I was summoned to a protest meeting of the elected officials of Allegheny County. They were hot. Lots of table-pounding and predictions of defeat. After giving them all a chance to vent their anger, I finally just said: "Look, Mark Singel is my running mate. He's going to *stay* my running mate. And that's that. You're supposed to be leaders. Start leading and stop whining about losing. Tell me how we're going to win. Let's pull together and let's move forward."

And that is what they did. The griping finally subsided, and the campaign began in earnest.

The primary against Rendell was a Texas death match—no holds-barred. I'll spare the details except to say that I had learned from bitter experience. When we heard Rendell had made a huge purchase of air time, or had just received a hefty contribution, or whatever, we didn't let ourselves get rattled. We stuck to our game plan and stayed with our message. Each time we were tagged, we swung back.

We were very concerned about the Flaherty challenge to Singel. We had to devise a specific strategy to deal with the problem: to give Mark Singel maximum visibility and let the people know we were the Casey-Singel ticket. That we were running as a team.

So Bob Shrum and our consultants put their heads together and came up with a simple but ingenious TV spot built around famed New York Yankee manager Casey Stengel. Just about everyone in Pennsylvania knew the name, Casey Stengel. So they prepared a TV spot which began with a picture of the Yankee legend and a voice-over saying, "You've all heard of Casey Stengel. Well, in the upcoming Democratic primary it's not Casey Stengel, it's Casey-Singel." We invested $350,000 in TV time to put Singel over the top, and it worked.

On primary election night, I was taking a shower on the second floor of our home in Scranton. As I stepped out of the shower I heard a commotion downstairs. Wrapped in a towel, I looked out to find Caddell charging up the stairs: "Singel's beating Flaherty in Pittsburgh—two to one!"

That meant it was in the bag. If he was winning by that margin in Flaherty's hometown, elsewhere Singel's margin was sure to be bigger. When the votes were counted we had beaten Rendell going away—57 percent to 41 percent. A solid victory. I had finally broken the primary election jinx.

Just a few years later, Ed Rendell would go on to become the popular mayor of Philadelphia. As governor I worked closely with him to help restore the city's fiscal stability, and to support a wide range of programs to help the city and its people. Once adversaries, we became strong allies.

Now I had an even tougher challenge ahead: the general election against Lieutenant Governor Bill Scranton.

"Like a novel by John O'Hara," said *Time* magazine, "this race stars two men from the same small city: William Worthington Scranton III, thirty-nine, scion of the state's most powerful political family, and Robert Patrick Casey, fifty-four, a tall, black-browed Irishman whose father once worked in the coal mines around Scranton. . . ."

No Scranton had ever lost an election in Pennsylvania. He had everything going for him. At thirty-one he'd been elected lieutenant governor. The Thornburgh administration was finishing strong. Raising money would not be a problem. The pundits were hailing Bill III as a voice of the future, a refreshing presence on the political scene with clear national prospects. He was pro-choice, "fiscally conservative but socially liberal." While the fur was flying between Rendell and me, Scranton was gliding along without any opposition in the Republican primary. About the only question in media circles was whether young Scranton would seek a second term as governor, and after that, who knew?

Even in my own family there were serious doubts about the very idea of taking on a Scranton. We still tell the story of Ellen's exchange with her aunt Clare.

"Well, he's going to run again," said Ellen.

"Oh," responded Clare. "For what?"

"Governor," said Ellen.

"Oh, that's nice," she replied pleasantly. "Who's he going to run against?"

"Bill Scranton."

"Bill Scranton!" Clare exclaimed. "He can *never* beat Bill Scranton!"

I was realistic about my own prospects, but not for any of the reasons I'd been reading in the press. None of these really troubled me. Except for his fund-raising, I regarded each of his perceived advantages as a liability to be exploited. Voters are not as impressed as reporters by "scions" and the like, least of all the voters of a working-class state like Pennsylvania. They don't like to be taken for granted. And there was something a little too confident about the Scranton campaign. I knew a lot of Pennsylvanians would see it that way too. I came from a pretty good family myself. I would tell our story. If Scranton wanted to make it a contest of family names, I would gladly run mine against his, and let the voters decide which better reflected their own experience and hopes for the future.

A story I heard after the election made the rounds in Scranton: An elderly gentleman of Irish descent explained the meaning of the election this way. "You know," he said, "for a hundred years they told us that shoveling the manure was as good as riding the horse."

"Well," he went on, "in 1986, when Casey ran, we decided to ride the horse."

Scranton took full advantage of his early momentum. He was raising an incredible amount of money, without even breaking a sweat. Every week there was a splash in the papers announcing another successful Scranton fund-raiser. One week it was James Baker in town to toast the next governor, the next week Henry Kissinger, the next week New Jersey Governor Tom Kean. In awe of these visiting stars, the media gave Scranton a decisive edge. I was impressed more by the money than the endorsements. People in Pittsburgh and York and Carbondale and Monessen were not going to ask themselves on Election Day which of these guys Henry Kissinger had endorsed.

To make matters worse, there was still the residue of bad feeling towards the Democrats because of corruption in the Shapp administration. The Republicans had been running against Shapp since he left office in 1978. Scranton was going to hit me with Shapp, never mind that I'd run against Shapp twice and had watched him like a hawk as auditor general. Soon Scranton began running negative television ads against me. I remember calling a friend of mine the first day I learned of the Scranton TV ads and saying to him: "Have you got your calendar handy? Draw a circle around today's date. This is the day Scranton went negative against me. Keep that date as a reference."

The Scranton strategy was transparent: Try to tie Casey to the corruption of the Shapp years, and in general to an older, seamier time in Pennsylvania politics. My primary victory, said Scranton, was "clearly a victory for the old politics," full of "unparalleled corruption. I'm not saying Bob Casey is a bum. But you are electing a party." Nothing subtle there. The issue was not whether I was a good candidate, but whether or not I was "a bum."

What really bothered me was that Governor Thornburgh knew I had cracked down hard on corruption in the Shapp administration when I was auditor general. One of our investigations had led to criminal charges against a top Shapp official. We had forwarded our findings to Thornburgh when he was U.S. Attorney for the Western District of Pennsylvania. Because the record clearly showed that I had fought Shapp at every turn, I was furious at Scranton's tactics. He knew better. He was publisher of a weekly newspaper which had endorsed me for reelection as auditor general. And he conveniently ignored the recent indictment of two prominent Republicans in a contract bribery scandal.

My problem was that, after going all out to win the primary against Rendell, my campaign was broke. So we could not answer the Scranton attacks. He had been attacking me for a solid month, and the attacks went unanswered. I knew from bitter experience what unanswered attacks can cost. By August, I was behind Scranton by fifteen points in our poll.

Politicians will tell you that you can't raise money in August because people are on vacation. Baloney. My daughter Kate and I got on the phone and raised a million dollars in the month of August 1986. And I was fifteen points down! I made up my mind that if Mr. Scranton was looking for a fight, he had come to the right place.

From there on, the '86 election was a Pier Six brawl. It's best remembered as a contest of TV ads. In September, Scranton made a million-dollar TV buy. But meanwhile our research team one day reported back with some astonishing facts. During his eight years as lieutenant governor, Scranton had been absent 84 percent of the time from the Senate sessions over which—as lieutenant governor—he was required to preside. He'd skipped 80 percent of the meetings of the State Pardons Board, of which he was chairman. And as chairman of the Pennsylvania Emergency Management Agency, he had a perfect record of 100 percent—he hadn't been to a single meeting.

"How can someone lead Pennsylvania into the future," said our TV spot, "if he doesn't go to work?" It was devastating.

Scranton protested that the ads were negative and unfair. I responded by saying: "The problem Scranton has is not negative television ads. His problem is his negative record. And he can't shield his record from public scrutiny. That's what elections are all about: the records of the candidates."

It was true, of course, that lieutenant governors routinely absent themselves from senate proceedings, turning the chair over to a president pro tempore in the manner of the vice president. We took the view that if the constitution said his job was to be there, presiding over the Senate, then that's exactly where he should have been. That was the job description. The same tradition, in any case, did not explain Scranton's chronic absence from meetings of the Pardons Board and Emergency Management Agency—two fairly important responsibilities. When Singel became lieutenant governor, he watched his attendance very carefully.

Gradually, we began closing in on Scranton, narrowing his lead. We were definitely within striking distance, and gaining momentum. And then, as the election moved into the home stretch and I was preparing for our statewide TV debate, Scranton made a dramatic move.

He announced that, after a weekend of reflection with his wife, the two of them were "disturbed by the tone of the campaign." The campaign, he said, had become a "back-alley brawl." He would now take the "high road" and swear off the negative campaigning.

August was not too far back in my memory, when I was broke, behind in the polls, and defenseless against Scranton's own attack ads. I lost no sleep over our ads. At all events the "high road" pledge was hailed by reporters and it helped his campaign. He began to recover lost ground in the polls, and increased his lead. It was a smart tactic. And we let several days go by without an effective response.

Then one Saturday afternoon shortly before the election, I was out campaigning in Pittsburgh when I got a call from Carville. "There's a woman in Clarks Summit who's telling us she received a political brochure from Scranton in today's mail. The ad attacks you. It's a rough, negative hit piece."

A few calls later, Carville had a copy of the brochure. It was over the line: a personal attack accusing me, among other falsehoods, of being "blind to the fraud, abuse, and corruption" of the Shapp administration. What's more, the Scranton campaign had sent out six hundred thousand of them. Carville called Billy McGrath, my son-in-law, who worked for a printing company: "Billy, we need six hundred thousand envelopes by tomorrow." Without batting an eye, Billy said: "What color?"

The next day we held a press conference in downtown Scranton. Standing before a mountain of paper, I asked Scranton what had become of his noble "high road" pledge.

Scranton said he knew nothing about the mailing. It was all a terrible mistake. But he was not convincing. "How," I asked, "can he possibly not know that six hundred thousand brochures are being sent out all over the state in his name? How could he manage the state if he doesn't even know what's going on in his own campaign?"

Overnight, the momentum shifted in our favor. We began to close the gap again.

As Election Day approached, my campaign was divided over an ad our side had produced but not run. During the campaign Scranton, in response to a reporter's question, had admitted to "recreational drug use." Our ad showed an employment application for the police department. On it was a line asking applicants to disclose any drug involvement. Of course, admission of drug use disqualified one from any service in law enforcement. "If you can't serve on the police force because of drug usage," said a voice-over, "why should there be a different rule for someone who wants to be governor of Pennsylvania?"

Carville and I were against it. The ad had nothing to do with Scranton's record as a public official; it wasn't fair comment, and besides—he'd come clean. The whole thing would only backfire. But I was down five points in the polls and others in the campaign thought we should take the risk. After batting it around a while, one advisor turned to Carville and accused him of being "gun-shy" because of another controversial attack ad aired in one of Carville's losing campaigns. At that point I concluded the meeting: "This ad is not going to be used." And that ended it.

In short order our ad people returned with another idea. It was a matter of public record that prior to being elected lieutenant governor, Scranton had been involved with Transcendental Meditation. He had evangelized for TM all over the world as a disciple of the Maharishi Mahesh Yogi. He had worked for the TM organization for four years. He was featured in a news article in which he had announced that he wanted to bring TM into state government. Thus, it became a part of his record.

That was a hard one to pass up. Our ad showed a picture of the young disciple with long, scruffy hair. Next was a picture of the Maharishi Mahesh Yogi. Then a picture of the news article. In the background, sitar music to set the mood.

We decided to use the ad. It was, I felt, legitimate commentary on Scranton's record. Long after the election, pundits were still debating "the guru ad" and its effect. Most in the media jumped to the conclusion that the ad had finished off Scranton. This became the conventional wisdom, and a easy way of dismissing my victory, based only on unsubstantiated opinion.

Stung by the ad, Scranton staged a press conference bringing in his father and mother, former Governor Scranton and Mary Scranton, to denounce me. Fair or not, it left the impression that when things got rough he'd gone scurrying to Mom and Dad.

Before that press conference was over, we had dispatched my children across the state: Chris and Margi to Lancaster, Mary Ellen and Pat to Altoona, Kate and Matt to Scranton, Erin and Bobby to Erie. In each town, they went straight to the television studios, marching in to answer the Scrantons' attack on me. I will never forget Matt's finest moment. Picture it: A gray-haired, distinguished former Pennsylvania governor and the former first lady appear on your television screen to denounce me and accuse me of unfair campaign tactics. Then a boy of high-school age, my youngest son, Matt, comes on to say, "The attack on my father is unjustified. All he is doing is holding Scranton accountable for his record. A candidate's record is always an issue in a political campaign."

In the closing days, the Republicans hit me with their big guns—all at once. Voters could receive a recorded personal plea to vote for Scranton from President Ronald Reagan by merely dialing a toll-free telephone number. Scranton also aired a TV ad in which the president endorsed him. The airwaves were full of pro-Scranton commercials, featuring Senator John Heinz, Governor Thornburgh and, of course, former Governor Scranton. I must confess that I was concerned about the effect of this closing barrage of endorsements. I had never seen anything like it before or since in Pennsylvania. We went into Election Day with the race declared too close to call, a statistical dead heat.

My concern deepened with each passing hour on Election Day. Bob Shrum had received the results of so-called exit polling—a sampling of actual votes cast in key precincts—from a friend of his at one of the networks. And they showed us slipping. Not a good sign.

That night our house was jam packed. Friends, neighbors, campaign people, and family wall to wall. Every few minutes when new reports came in, there would be this deep silence, everybody leaning forward to the TV, freezing in place. Then came a collective gasp of relief or alarm.

It's a happy memory now, but at the time the suspense was awful. This was it for me. Life would go on if I lost; my wife and family would keep loving me; Pennsylvania would survive without me as governor. I had fought my fight, done my best. But true as they are, those are comforting thoughts we cling to in defeat. At the end of the day, there would be no escaping the pain of losing. I didn't want philosophical consolations this time. I'd had my fill of them. At the moment it seemed less an election than a verdict on my whole life. I didn't want to go down as a four-time loser, a valiant contender, an also-ran in the Scranton Saga. I wanted to win.

When the tension had become almost intolerable for us all, Carville began working the phone in search of new scraps of information. In the kitchen, everybody was trying to change the channel, flipping from NBC to CBS to ABC and back again. Around 9:30 or 10:00 P.M., we heard from a neighbor that ABC had just called me the winner, setting off a frenzy of channel-changing. About an hour later, NBC called me the winner. But what about CBS? They were holding out. Maybe something had gone wrong! We turned to CBS and waited: "In Pennsylvania, it is still too close to call."

Around midnight we heard CBS anchor Dan Rather's voice: "In Pennsylvania, upset for the Democrats!

"Lieutenant Governor William Scranton III, the son of the former governor of Pennsylvania, and a favored Republican to follow on to the Republican governor Richard Thornburgh . . . has *lost* to attorney Bob Casey! According to our CBS News estimate, Bob Casey will be the new Democratic governor of Pennsylvania. Big upset there."

I had been upstairs getting dressed. As I heard Rather's voice, I came down the steps. I got to the kitchen just after he said I'd won. I hugged Ellen, and then my son Pat. It was over.

Bill Scranton III gave a concession speech in which he mentioned my name, but never made the obligatory phone call to congratulate me that night. To this day, I have never heard from him. No one knows better than I do how hard it is to lose.

And I'm sure the loss fell very heavily on the Scranton family. Despite this, Governor Scranton wrote me a letter of congratulations shortly after the election. And not long after my transplant operation, Ellen and I received a very warm and generous letter from Governor Scranton. It was the mark of a big man.

Bachrach

My father, Alphonsus L. Casey.

Russell McElroy

With my brother,
John (left).

Holy Cross vs. St. Johns, played at Madison Square Garden in 1953.
I'm number 35 for Holy Cross.

Holy Cross College
yearbook—1953.

Mother and Dad with our oldest daughter, Margi.

This family photo was taken during my 1962
State Senate campaign.

First-term state senator swearing-in January 1963.

Campaign photo of the Caseys taken in 1966.

Stanley Olds, Scranton

Associated Press / Wide World Photo

With Ellen, at a press conference announcing my 1966 candidacy for governor.

Speaking at the Pennsylvania Constitutional Convention in 1967. Far left is Lieutenant Governor Raymond J. Broderick; second from right is Frank A. Orban Jr., Esquire; at right is author James A. Michener.

Swearing in as auditor general by Federal Judge William J. Nealon—May 1969.

Swearing in as auditor general for the second term in 1973, Judge Nealon presiding.

Campaign kickoff for my 1978 bid for governor.

With my opponent
Lieutenant Governor
William Scranton during
a 1986 gubernatorial
campaign debate.

Primary election night—May 1986 in Scranton.

Associated Press / Wide World Photo

Victory! General Election night in Scranton—November 1986. We won!

Commonwealth Media Services

Sworn in as Pennsylvania's governor by Pennsylvania Chief Justice Robert N. C. Nix, Jr. on January 20, 1987; outgoing Governor Dick Thornburgh looking on.

Dancing with Ellen at the Inaugural Ball.

In the library of the Pennsylvania Governor's Residence — Harrisburg.

Speedwalking on October 1, 1988 near the governor's residence, flanked by state troopers.

Cleaning up Pennsylvania—another campaign commitment kept.

Recuperating from heart bypass surgery—
October 1987.

Announcing my candidacy for reelection as governor with Lieutenant
Governor Mark Singel—March 1990.

Signing the contract to begin the Children's Health Insurance program
in Harrisburg—May 1993.

With Frances Lucas in Monessen—1994.

Back to work after double-transplant surgery. Son Matt gives me the "high five" as Ellen (left) and daughter Margi (right) applaud—December 21, 1993.

Casey Family Archives

The Casey family at our summer home in Lake Ariel, Pennsylvania — 1994.

11

Strangers

Death is the Great Leveler. Different as our lives were, at that moment Michael Lucas and I were nothing more or less than two broken people in need.

WAITING FOR his story to be told is the young man whose heart and liver saved me—Michael Lucas.

It was out in the waiting room, during the transplant, that my family first heard his name. Soon people across America would hear it. My operation was still going on, but already the reporters had somehow pieced the whole story together. There were a week's worth of reports that I'd jumped the line of transplant recipients. These were false (normal procedures had been observed to the letter), and when the media dropped that angle, Michael Lucas's picture and name soon passed from the screen, making way for stories about my regaining consciousness, recovering, walking, reassuming power.

In a way, that was Michael Lucas's life story. He was one of those people whose lives come to public attention only when they meet a violent end—people we never see until their names turn up in the newspaper or on the television screen. Most remarkable to me is that he came from Monessen—the town I'd visited as a symbol of my

commitment to Pennsylvania's economic rebirth. And more than a symbol: a real place full of people in need of help. I've told the story of the
1986 campaign as a personal one, a milestone in my own life. But of
course, in the big picture, that story of personal comebacks and dueling
campaigns was not much more than a footnote to what was happening
in Pennsylvania. What was happening can better be seen in Monessen,
in Michael Lucas's life and how it came together with mine.

This is what really stays with me from my whole ordeal, the mystery—there may be a better word, but I can't think of it —of being saved
by complete strangers. When you stop to think about it, it happens all
the time. None of us could begin to count the debts we owe to people
we never met, let alone those we do know. In my case, all the debts
seemed to appear in an instant, one person after another stepping in to
cover them for me.

I had spent many years trying to become the highest official in the
state—with the usual mix of good intention and sheer ambition. According to the script, I was the public servant, the big shot out there helping
others, the governor, the one with power. All that vanished in a flash. I
was in trouble. No more illusions about power and control: I was as helpless as a child. Through no merit of my own, no title or office or anything
else, I was surrounded by strangers trying to save me. All went well beyond the duties of their profession. Around the state were more strangers
praying for me, not as their governor or partisan leader but as a fellow
human being in need. In a hospital room not far from mine was Mrs.
Frances Lucas, who had just seen her son die. With one hard choice, she
rescued me. Sometimes I think there was a design to it all, that I was
thrown down from my little seat of power back to complete dependency,
maybe for a another glimpse of how the world looks from there.

Michael Lucas's life and mine began winding
together with a knock on the back door of the Lucas house Sunday
evening, June 6, 1993. Standing there in front of Lucas, he recognized
a young friend. From out of nowhere, a stranger appeared and pointed
a gun at him, barking orders. A moment later he was fighting for his life

life against a mob of strangers. They were drug dealers looking for stolen goods. But it was all a case of mistaken identity. Wrong place, wrong guy.

His mother, Frances Lucas, worked at the area hospital. She came home from work that night to find Michael's hat and one of his shoes lying in the street. She followed a blood trail up the front steps. Inside the house stood Michael, a blood-soaked towel around his head. The police had arrived. But for some reason, no ambulance.

Frances rushed him back to the hospital she'd just left. Twice during that ride, she had to stop to revive him. The story as it's been recounted to me is hard to bear. "Why did they do this?" Michael kept asking on the ride to the hospital. "Why did they do this, Mama?"

At the hospital, tests were quickly taken of Michael's brain. It was hemorrhaging. As he was airlifted to the area's major trauma center, Allegheny General Hospital, neurosurgeons prepared to operate on his brain. "Why did they do this to me? Why?" Shortly after surgery, he slipped into a coma. At 6:31 P.M. on Saturday, June 13, while I lay in my hospital bed across town waiting for the results of my cardiac tests, William Michael Lucas died.

About Michael Lucas, I know only what I've read and heard from those who knew him. Our lives couldn't have been any more different. He was in his thirties; I was in my sixties. He was black; I was white. We did have one thing in common. He was the son of a steel worker; my father had worked in the coal mines. I was raised in what used to be the anthracite coal region of Pennsylvania; he grew up in the steel area, both of which had at one time attracted people from across the world to create America's Industrial Age.

But then the coal gave out and the steel industry collapsed. Monessen had been dominated by the Wheeling Pittsburgh Steel Plant which stretched for what seemed miles along the road entering the town. Most everyone worked there, generation after generation, until without much notice the mill shut down.

The Lucas family had once sat securely among the middle class of Monessen. When things turned bad, their fortunes followed. Michael struggled. He went from job to job, moving finally to Washington,

D.C., for a position he thought would be his future. Then he was laid off. The big mistake of his life came when he turned to crack cocaine. But his family didn't give up on him. His sister and mother went to Washington and brought him back home.

He'd begun to shake off the despair and stage a comeback of his own. It was that effort that brought him to the job training center I had visited in Monessen weeks before my transplant. He applied for over a hundred jobs, but in Monessen at the time even college graduates were lucky to find work.

From there, the man's life story moves back into the clipped terms of a police report—"young black male killed in drug-related incident." That friend who showed up at Michael's door had been dealing in cocaine. He was in trouble, hunted by suppliers to whom he owed ten thousand dollars. So, police believe, he fabricated a story involving Mike Lucas: Michael's nephew, he said, had taken the drugs, and Michael Lucas knew where they were.

Thirteen men have been charged with the Lucas murder. One was found guilty in May 1994 and was sentenced to serve ten to twenty years in prison. The twelve others were awaiting trial in state court in Westmoreland County—with proceedings expected to conclude by summer 1996. In addition, eight of these individuals faced related federal charges for conspiracy to distribute narcotics and engage in money laundering in the Federal District Court for the Western District of Pennsylvania.

In Frances Lucas, I met one of the finest people I've ever known. In the space of an hour that summer, she lost a son and saved a stranger with a grace that will always amaze me. As if that weren't enough, her oldest son, Eugene, had been the victim of another murder. Eugene was shot in the back while Michael was still in high school. When they asked Mrs. Lucas whether she would agree to donate Michael's organs, she said simply: "Michael had a good heart. It would be right for someone else to have it."

For me, of course, it feels very strange to tell this story. What do you say about a man you never knew, whose violent death gave you new life? You can say, "It's a mystery," and go on trying to live your life in a grateful way. You can offer up prayers for the guy on the other side of the big scale. But it will never be enough. For me, there will always be some things beyond my understanding—questions like Michael Lucas was asking with his last breath: "Why?" Here was a young man who needed a break at least as much as I did. Why did my deliverance have to mean his death?

I don't know the whole answer—I never will—but I do know part of it: At the moment of death we are all the same. Death is the Great Leveler. Different as our lives were, at that moment Michael Lucas and I were nothing more or less than two broken people in need. Our color, class, or any other categories the world might invent to separate us, all at that instant were equally meaningless; our parts, literally, were interchangeable. When I was dying, I didn't ask the color of the donor's skin, and when she was signing the document to donate Michael's organs, Mrs. Lucas didn't ask the color of the recipient. We were all just people in trouble and pain, left with nothing but our own humanity.

It had been about seven hours since Ellen and I parted at the entrance to the operating room when all of a sudden she looked up to find Dr. John Armitage, his arms outstretched. "How 'bout a hug?"

With Dr. Si M. Pham, he had just finished my heart transplant—the first of a two-part operation. The heart was in, he told Ellen, and the procedure had been "flawless." "This," he said, banging a fist on the door, "was how hard your husband's heart was."

Then Jeff Romoff, chief executive officer of the hospital, came in to the room. An experienced professional, he had seen all kinds of operations and medical procedures. He had watched the moment when Michael Lucas's heart was given its first surge of blood, a moment when the new heart would either begin to beat again, or not: the moment of truth. He had seen many heart transplants; never, he said, had he seen anything like this. "Usually we have to pump the heart to get it started.

We just *touched* it with blood, and it began to beat like a trip hammer," said Romoff. Then he began to cry.

The liver transplant team took over: Dr. Satoru Todo, Dr. John Fung, Dr. Jorge Reyes, and Dr. Roderick Stevenson worked to disconnect each blood vessel attaching my old liver to the other abdominal organs through which the liver provides more than five hundred functions for the human body. They connected each of those organs to Michael Lucas's liver. This stage alone took about eight-and-a-half hours. Then another moment of truth—a surge of blood through my system. They unclasped the vessel holding back the heart's flow of blood and waited. Suddenly the transplanted liver turned from gray to pink, coming alive in my body.

When my eyes opened at three in the morning, some eleven or twelve hours ahead of schedule, I felt like a man ensnared in a trap. Tubes and wires were criss-crossing my swollen body. All around me, a team of doctors and nurses in the intensive care unit ministered to me. I felt myself carried in and out of consciousness by the lingering anesthesia, up and down, more and more gently, as on a wave, until, finally, I was ashore. Standing above me, I saw Dr. Starzl. I tried to speak but couldn't because of the tubes. With all my power, I raised my arm and touched his face.

12

Details

*Brothers and sisters do not speak of "wagons" and "loads"
and "burdens." Isn't that what we are in the end–brothers
and sisters in the human family–every last one of us in need
of the other?*

THE PENNSYLVANIA governor's residence was only the third house
Ellen and I had ever lived in. The bigness of it took a little getting used
to. With all the exquisite paintings and antique furniture, moving into
the governor's residence was like moving into a museum. But having
more than one shower—that was a joy Ellen and I had never known,
and alone seemed to justify all the struggles we'd been through to get
there. But every chance we got, we spent weekends and holidays in our
house in Scranton, our only real home.

On the night before my first inauguration, it had snowed heavily.
When I stood up to deliver my address, I felt like the new governor of
Alaska; everything was blanketed in ice and snow. After the inaugural
celebrations, it was on to Monessen for my long-promised appearance
there.

I'm not a political philosopher. In all the years I sought and held
public office, I have never recorded my political philosophy in any sys-
tematic way. But I was clear about the absolute need to help areas hard

hit by economic change: Here was Monessen, and towns like it across Pennsylvania. They were going through a time very similar to what I had witnessed as a boy growing up in coal country. When coal died, our people suffered. Now the steel industry was dying. Entire factories had vanished, rendering the skills and work experience of those workers, the only work skills they had, all but useless. Working families were devastated.

Sitting back as governor and waiting for better times was not an option. These towns were not going to spring back to life all by themselves, through some inexorable turn of the economic cycle. Even if the cycle did eventually come around to help, there were a lot of people who would be unable to wait it out.

Our response was to help them, using all the power of the Commonwealth of Pennsylvania. The economic development plan we offered during the campaign — the fruit of many hours of planning and discussion with Mike Hershock and his associates, Steve Rosskopf, and Lori Fehr — gave priority consideration to devastated areas like Monessen. And I was determined to follow it. We set up job training centers in Monessen and other towns. For many people, this was the break they'd been waiting for. We invested in infrastructure — roads, highways, bridges, water and sewage systems. We joined with the private sector to invest in economic growth to create new jobs. In many cases, these efforts wouldn't pay off until years later, in growth that perhaps we would not live to see.

The depth of my determination to help families in areas of our state suffering economic hardship, in western Pennsylvania or anywhere else, was dramatized by my visit to Monessen the very day after my first inauguration. And I knew the people understood full well the significance of that visit. Looking back, I know my administration did our best to deliver on our promises by investing in these regions which had been neglected in the past.

Using government to help people in trouble just seemed to me the most obvious thing in the world. Of course, I knew there were limits to what government could do. And of course, there were constitutional limits to what it should even attempt to do.

I have as little faith in a society managed at every turn by government planners as I do a society left entirely to the caprice of market forces. Ours is a free-market system based upon the efforts, ideas, and initiative of individuals. To that, we owe a general prosperity found nowhere else on earth. But the system has a lot of rough spots and deep-cutting edges. In any free society there will always be people who are vulnerable, at the mercy of those with power. In the name of "freedom," we cannot sit back and let some people be trampled by others. We cannot let the weak be exploited by the strong.

Only government, when all else fails, can safeguard the vulnerable and powerless. When it renegs on that obligation, freedom becomes a hollow word. A hard-working person unable to find work and support his or her family is not free. A person for whom sickness means financial ruin, with no health insurance to soften the blow, is not free. A malnourished child, an uneducated child, a child trapped in foster care—these children are not free. And without a few breaks along the way from government, such children in most cases will never be truly free.

"Without justice, what are kingdoms but great bands of robbers?" St. Augustine asked. I believe the most important quality a person can bring to political office is a passion for justice and sense of outrage in the face of injustice. If you can pass lightly over wrongs done to your neighbor, if you can shrug off the suffering of others—especially children—then you are miscast for any position of public responsibility. You should return to private pursuits where less is expected of you. You're in the wrong business.

If you once had that sense of outrage and lost it somewhere along your climb to power, you're finished—done for. No matter how far up you climb, you'll have lost your bearings. I have seen all too many politicians like this. They're like parts in search of a play, running back and forth in vain attempts to please everyone, living for the sound of the applause. In the end, no matter how high they go, they depart the public stage in a general atmosphere of disappointment and bewilderment. What they've lost is much more important and satisfying than applause. Politically, they've gained the world and lost their souls.

Indifference to people in need has always struck me as a much deeper threat to freedom than outright evil. Indifference is the attitude that simply walks away from every complex problem; the attitude that says, "Let others take care of it. It's their problem. Personally I'm opposed to it, but . . ." It is the modern version of, "Am I my brother's keeper?"

I do not believe that every moral duty can or should be entrusted to government. But I am dead-certain that when people are in serious trouble—unemployed, exploited, forgotten by the rest of society—it is government's duty to protect them. And those people should not be viewed as a burden to the rest of us: they are our neighbors, our fellow citizens. If each of us—even the most affluent and independent among us—were to take an honest look in the mirror, we would see people just like them, people entirely dependent on the help, encouragement, goodwill, and forbearance of others.

Lately I've been hearing one of the Republican candidates for president talking about throwing people off "the wagon" and making them help with the pulling for a change. What a sad view of America, of life itself! Who among us has not spent some time in that "wagon," borne along by the strength of others, unable for some reason or by some circumstance to walk the full distance? I sure have. I would not be alive but for the kindness, compassion, and generosity—heroic generosity—of people around me. Brothers and sisters do not speak of "wagons" and "loads" and "burdens." Isn't that what we are in the end—brothers and sisters in the human family—every last one of us in need of the other?

This is why I don't go along with some Republican leaders who today dismiss the very idea that government has a fundamental obligation to help the jobless, the sick, the homeless. Such sweeping skepticism is the luxury of those who have never stood in an unemployment line or slept in a public shelter. I could show them entire communities in Pennsylvania that would hardly have survived the last twenty years without the help of government. I could introduce them to people who today would be jobless, on the street, or in a state penitentiary if government had not been there when they needed help.

In the same way, it's all well and good to declare that America is a land of equal opportunity for all. But as a practical matter, you have to

prove it in your own conduct. As governor I wanted to be a strong witness for equal rights for all people and all groups in society. I'm proud,
for example, that over half of all African-American cabinet officers since
Pennsylvania was founded were appointed during the years I was governor. I appointed eleven African-American cabinet members in just eight
years as governor, including the first state police commissioner and the
first commissioner of corrections. I appointed the first black woman to
the state Supreme Court—also a first for the nation.

Conservatives, though, do have a point about some functions of government, and I think it accounts in part for their electoral success in
1994. In fact, America has only rediscovered an old truth—that power's
reach is often greater than its grasp. It's clear to most members of both
parties that all the money in the world will not solve America's deeper
social problems, and that good intentions alone do not make for Great
Societies.

I wanted my administration to offer a truly activist government, with
everybody keeping their eyes on the original goals in all their simplicity. I didn't want us to merely settle in and keep state government on
cruise control. I went into office believing in limited government and
unlimited opportunity for individuals. But I also held a strong belief that
government could help make life better for ordinary people.

Sometimes this vision translated into a reduction in government and
lower taxes. For instance, we cut business taxes several times. That left
more money for business people to invest in their enterprises and hire
more workers. And we enacted the toughest laws in the nation to guard
against the corporate raiders of the 1980s. A lot of jobs were being lost,
and families and communities destroyed by corporate raiding, and only
government could protect them. In fact, the heads of Pennsylvania corporations—normally cool to the idea of government intervention in the
free market—were eager for me to put a stop to corporate raiding because their companies were likely candidates for hostile takeovers.

At the same time, we reduced the tax burden for working families on
four separate occasions by reducing the state personal income tax. I
have always found something perverse in the way working families
across America are treated by our federal tax codes, and I tried to relieve

the burden as much as possible in Pennsylvania's state code. Federal tax laws seem almost deliberately designed to drive families apart. Working families today produce two-thirds of America's gross domestic product, but they bear four-fifths of the federal tax burden. And they do not have teams of accountants to finesse and massage their tax bills for them. Why, for instance, is the money spent to feed, clothe, and educate your children called "consumption," and therefore taxable, while money you spend on a building or piece of machinery is called "investment" and can be written off? Isn't investment in children and families just as important to America as investment in buildings and machines? Some would say it's *more important*, and I am one of them.

Across America each morning, mothers go off in one direction, fathers go off in another, and the children go off to daycare. Our tax laws are almost entirely indifferent to the hardships of supporting children. Working parents must spend more and more time being breadwinners—with less and less bread to show for it. The more they work, the less time they have for the greatest work of all: parenting.

As governor, I tried to put *family formation* on par with *capital formation*. Wherever government could encourage or assist working families, lightening their loads a little, my administration did it.

Pennsylvania, during my term, ranked number one in collecting child support from deadbeat dads. While cutting some programs that weren't working, we built upon others that were—child nutrition programs, prenatal healthcare, health insurance for children, and early intervention programs to help developmentally delayed children. We also tried to encourage private initiative instead of stepping in with all-out state involvement, as in our Aid to the Caregiver program, which helped family members caring for an elderly relative at home. In each case it was a minimal involvement by government in people's lives, but an absolutely vital one.

Another benefit to working families came from our program to reduce the runaway cost of auto insurance. We saved drivers billions of dollars by reforming the system. Insurance rates had been going up about 20 percent a year. To bring rates down and make it stick in the courts (we were sued over a hundred times and won every case) we had to take on three of the most powerful lobbies in the country: the trial lawyers, the medical society, and the insurance industry. I count our auto insurance reforms as among the best things we did that first term. It's an excellent example of how an activist government can relieve people's burdens without unduly interfering in their lives.

The same goes for our environmental reforms. Our biggest effort here was legislation I proposed to establish the largest and most successful recycling and clean-water programs in the country. As of 1986, Pennsylvania led the nation in the incidence of water-borne disease. In northeastern Pennsylvania, in Altoona and McKeesport, people had to boil their drinking water. Many people contracted giardiasis, a stomach ailment, from the contaminated water. The problem arose from unprotected surface reservoirs where the water was stored. Some water utilities had not installed filtration systems. We levied a fine of $350,000 on the Pennsylvania Gas & Water Company because their water was dirty—the largest fine ever imposed on a public utility. But we also helped the same company finance the building of filtration systems. The issue figured in the 1986 election when I charged my opponent, Lieutenant Governor Scranton, of doing nothing to address the problem. Paul Begala's description of Scranton's position, which we gave the press, was masterful: "Let them drink Perrier!"

Another way I tried to make good my pledge to help working families was to intervene, when I felt it necessary, in labor disputes. My general policy was to foster labor-management cooperation. My specific policy was, when disputes seemed intractable, to intervene personally and bring the weight of the governor's office to bear. In 1987, for example, there was a bitter dispute in the Lehigh Valley at Mack Truck. The company threatened to close the plant entirely and move to South Carolina. I went to Allentown and met with both sides, management of Mack and local and international representatives of the United Auto Workers. As a last resort, I got both sides to agree to bring in the well-known mediator, William Usery. In the end, the Allentown Mack Truck plant stayed in our state and hundreds of jobs were saved.

A more dramatic situation was the dispute at Cooper Industries in Canonsburg, in Washington County near Pittsburgh, in October 1991.

The company had announced publicly that a decision had been made, and it was final: the Canonsburg plant would be closed. This decision came after a long period of wrangling between the company and the United Steelworkers Union. The heart of the dispute was the workers' healthcare plan, what medical coverage it would provide, and whether the company or the workers would pay for it.

I decided to make a last-ditch effort to save the thousand jobs that were about to be lost. Cooper Industries was the largest industrial employer in the county. I called Robert Cizik, CEO of Cooper in Dallas, Texas, and invited him to come to my office for face-to-face negotiations with Lynn Williams, international president of the Steelworkers Union. He agreed and came immediately to Harrisburg.

We all met in my office at 6:00 P.M. on October 14. At the outset, I told both sides: "Pennsylvania cannot afford to lose these jobs. There has to be a way to resolve this thing." At that point there didn't seem to be much hope. But we got right into it — all night long. Twelve intense hours of arguing, debating, proposals and counter-proposals. When the two sides would reach an impasse, they would come back to my office, and we'd kick it back and forth until the deadlock had been broken. Then they went back to the table for more negotiations. At dawn, Mr. Cizik and Lynn Williams announced they'd reached agreement. (In the course of our conversations, Cizik and I had discovered we had something in common. It turned out he was from Scranton and had lived there as a boy. His father had worked in the anthracite coal mines nearby.)

Throughout my time in office I also took a firm position against any expansion of gambling in Pennsylvania. For example, I vetoed a bill establishing off-track betting, though my veto was overridden — one of few such overrides during my two terms. We had better luck opposing the legalization of riverboat gambling in Pennsylvania. Just as other states were seizing upon riverboat gambling as a means of raising revenue without having to impose taxes, I opposed all such efforts, arguing that gambling as a revenue producer was "fool's gold": the estimates of revenue are almost always overstated. And the "jobs" created by gambling are not the kind that produce wages high enough to support families, not the kind of "jobs" government ought to be encouraging. Besides, gambling destroys families and the work ethic upon which they depend.

Those were among my successes as governor. But having noted them, I should also own up to at least one major failure. Politically, perhaps my biggest failure came at the very outset.

In 1987 we tried our hand at tax reform. Pennsylvania homeowners carried a heavy burden of real estate taxes. Pennsylvania is second only to Florida among all the states in the number of older citizens—and it meant the tax fell especially heavily on older citizens living on fixed incomes. Most of these property owners had paid off mortgages after many years of work and sacrifice. And, of course, their children were long since grown and no longer in school. And yet, by far the biggest chunk of the tax bill on real estate went to pay for the school system. Older people, who earlier paid taxes for the education of their children, were forced into bearing more and more school taxes.

State officials had been debating tax reform for years, casting about for a school finance system less dependent upon the real estate tax. Any governor taking on this issue assumed a huge political risk, either way. Win or lose. If you lost, you failed publicly before the entire state. If you prevailed, and the system was changed, you ran the risk of a backlash by those dissatisfied with the increased cost to them.

We lost. After a razor-thin, late-night legislative victory in the Republican Senate, made possible by the political courage of several senators crossing party lines, the issue was sent to the people in a statewide referendum to accept or reject the plan. I threw the full weight of my office behind it. I raised several hundred thousand dollars to urge a yes vote. As the election drew near, many of those officials who had initially supported the plan suddenly fell silent. They were feeling the political heat of the opposition—driven, I believed, by a fear of the unknown. The plan was complex, and we could not seem to get across its good points. When the votes were cast, the people rejected the plan by 80 percent to 20 percent.

The defeat was stunning. My standing in the polls plummeted. The political vultures began to circle. If I could not reverse this slide, my re-election prospects would be slim.

We had set aside $125 million to help local communities make the transition to new taxing systems in the event our tax reform plan was approved by the people. After the plan was defeated, I decided to press aggressively for a program to combat drugs and drug-related crime in Pennsylvania. Crack cocaine was just beginning to appear in Pennsylvania: The state police needed help in prosecuting the higher-ups in the drug trade. Local governments did not have the resources to fight the problem. There was a compelling need for anti-drug education in the schools, and support for programs offering the prospect of permanent recovery from chemical dependency was desperately needed.

With the state attorney general, state police commissioner, and members of my cabinet, I conducted a series of public hearings across the state, often running an entire work day. High-school children, police officers, recovered drug addicts, medical professionals, family members of addicts—dozens of ordinary citizens who were living witnesses to the drug scourge told their stories. The hearings totaled nearly one hundred hours of often compelling testimony, all recorded on television.

Armed with this evidence of the need for swift state action, we returned to Harrisburg and presented a report to the people and the legislature. We followed up with a thorough legislative program against drugs, a three-pronged counter-attack consisting of stronger law enforcement, increased education, and better drug treatment. State and local law-enforcement agencies were given funding for the first time for police officers—as well as "buy money" to be used to build prosecution cases against drug dealers, and also money for new and sophisticated law-enforcement technology. All in all, we were able to convince the legislature to appropriate ninety million dollars for our anti-drug program. It was a significant victory and, in political terms, a resounding comeback—after the tax reform defeat, showing political resilience and a capacity to set the terms of public debate, move public opinion, and have a divided legislature respond in a positive way.

13

Hard Cases

I will never forget a letter I received from a little girl in Hollsopple, Pennsylvania, a small town in Somerset County. When I packed up and left Harrisburg after my second term, it was among my most prized possessions.

WHEN ELECTION TIME rolled around in 1990, the air was filled with talk about my "vulnerability." By then most of the political hangover from tax reform had abated. Mostly, the negative talk had to do with my pro-life position. The *Webster* case, upholding limitations on the right to an abortion, had come down from the Supreme Court a year earlier. Supposedly, as the pundits and the media saw it, this would bring a terrible vengeance down upon pro-life office-holders across the land.

As governor, I viewed abortion as the gravest of a whole array of children's issues. For me, it was a simple step in logic: If government had a duty to protect the powerless, then who among us was the most powerless, most defenseless, most voiceless? The answer: Children.

All around the state were the children of poor families, uninsured and vulnerable to sickness and, in extreme cases, premature death. So we set up a program just for them, providing health insurance for poor children. The coverage provided virtually every service a child would need. When I left office, nearly fifty thousand children had been enrolled in the program. But it was only a good beginning, because many thousands of children remain uninsured.

All over Pennsylvania were children whose families could not afford a college education. So, as a state senator back in the 1960s, I had helped establish Pennsylvania's first scholarship program. As governor, I doubled the state's investment in scholarships, and we sent the aid directly to those families, avoiding a needless and costly bureaucracy.

Around the state were children caught in a nightmarish foster-care system. So we set up a statewide adoption network, helping them to find real homes and a real chance to make it in life. Among these were retarded children, minority children, and sibling groups likely to be broken off into different families. These were children with special needs.

What do you do with such "hard cases"? An easy question: You put them first in line.

That's what we did—we gave them priority. Far from these special-needs children being a burden, they were an urgent priority—their special needs our special duty.

It's almost a cliché these days for politicians to speak of the child, to end every speech by invoking "our children, and our children's children." To my ear, often there's a ring of meaningless sentimentality to these calls to action. The speaker might in one breath exhort us to remember the children, and our children's children, and in the next breath display utter indifference to the unborn. And not just indifference, but an attitude bordering on contempt for anyone who might intrude into the sentimental discussion by raising the problem of abortion, and what it reflects about our actual regard for children.

With each of my initiatives in Pennsylvania, fellow Democratic leaders at the national level would agree without reservation. Somehow, for reasons deeply mysterious to me, they cannot or will not see the connection between children's rights and abortion. To me, it is the most obvious connection in the world. Not to see it requires a monumental act of denial.

I could never understand how people could decry the serious problem of low birthweight infants and infant mortality on the one hand, and on the other hand argue that the unborn child could be aborted at will.

Should we not, as a caring society, protect the child in all these situations? By what logic does infant mortality become a concern to society only the moment after birth, but not the moment before?

We can talk on and on about the problems facing children: abusive parents, malnourishment, neglect. But almost always these social ills are just signs of a deeper malady. I would even say that in our culture today there is a callousness, a meanness, toward the child—a violent streak slowly spreading out across society. Let me say it directly: Abortion is the ultimate violence.

We worry today about the social problem of violence. We read of abandoned children, abused children, children molested or killed, children themselves committing acts of violence. Where did this spirit come from? How is it possible? How has life come to seem so cheap? I believe it's not only possible, it's inevitable. If a child in the womb, the most innocent thing on earth, is not safe—then who is? If as a nation we don't revere that child, that innocence, what will make us revere any life?

As a cultural phenomenon, maybe it all has something to do with the very innocence and helplessness of children. A child makes demands upon us. A child needs our constant attention. A child calls us beyond ourselves, beyond our wants and desires. In this way children are the natural enemy of a culture inclined more and more to worship the Imperial Self—to hide, deny, or dispose of anything which interferes with our own wishes and whims. This is especially true of the special-needs child, the child not up to our worldly standards of health, beauty, or general acceptability.

At some point my own party, once devoted to lifting up the powerless, bought into this idea. We still hear the same noble-sounding phrases— "compassion," "social justice," "equal rights." But they ring more and more hollow. In the abortion debate, they are thin veils concealing visions of raw self-interest. Who ever envisioned that the banner of "equal rights" would be unfurled over the abortion clinic? Who expected that we would ever even *think* of a mother and a child as having separate interests, as rivals in a dispute over power, much less enshrine the idea into law? Who ever imagined a political debate pitting mother against child, as if the child were some alien presence and not of her own flesh and blood?

Surely no two human beings could be more bound together, more natural allies in life and love than a mother and her baby. So infants were always viewed by humanity, especially by women themselves, at most times in most places—until our time, when suddenly we find them driven apart, when the maternal instinct to nurture and protect the child is turned on its head.

Everything depends on that tie of love. Sever it, and you have not only set in motion countless little tragedies, you put society itself on a short route to chaos. The cause of this division is an ethic of pure selfishness which has seeped into our political lives, the "me-first" ethic my party has embraced and which will prove its own undoing. It is modern liberalism's new and improved version of the old "rugged individualism" of Republicans: "Forget the powerless, forget the needs of others. *Me first!*"

As night follows day, violence follows this attitude. Whatever the pretenses, it is a hard creed, foreign to everything my party once stood for. You can see this in the strange terminology used in its defense. Even as the unborn child is sacrificed, the deed is dressed up in the language of love and concern, touching solicitude for the child's own "quality of life." A child, if born, will face hardship: therefore, he or she is better off dead. A baby will only burden one's economic situation, or require public assistance, or cause inconvenience all around: therefore, do everyone the favor of aborting it. Just get rid of it, and all will be well.

I may be putting it harshly, but that in the end is how such reasoning operates. All the talk we hear about children—all the "children's advocacy groups" and "Years of the Child"—seem almost another layer of denial, an appeasement of conscience by people who have turned their backs on the worst imaginable violence to children.

Republican leaders, in this respect, are not much better. In fact, both parties have come to resemble each other's worst caricature of the other. In both, we hear the same knack for casting raw self-interest in the language of altruism.

On the right, conservatives have captured the idealism of economic freedom. But often their idealism ends there. In other ways, they have embraced the spiritless vision of economic man—man in need of money alone. America has debated serious cultural problems—problems touching life, our duties to one another, the whole future of our country. And to each problem, some Republicans have offered the same answer: Money.

"I'm a fiscal conservative and a social liberal." We hear this more and more from Republicans. What is this ideology but the Imperial Self dressed up in a business suit? Money, like fire, is a very good thing when used properly. But it is a means and not an end. Money gives us freedom, which is good, but it does not incline our hearts to use that freedom wisely. It doesn't make us better people, better neighbors, better citizens, better parents. An ample bank account is no substitute for a well-informed conscience. No re-ordering of the tax code, no trimming of the budget, no amount of economic freedom will solve our society's deeper troubles.

The remarkable thing is that most Americans understand this. To hear party leaders hedging and wavering on the social issues, you would never guess that America is square in the middle of a social and cultural revolution, as I believe we are.

A generation's worth of experience with the self-gratification gospel has left most of us feeling a void, a deep emptiness in our culture. A generation's climb into general affluence has left us feeling somehow poorer as a nation. At the heart of our political debate today is a fear for our whole culture, a fear that something has gone terribly wrong. And it has. Try as we might to put it all out of our minds, at the heart of that unease is abortion—the ultimate act of violence, the ultimate exploitation of the weak by the powerful. A society, least of all a society like ours, cannot turn its back on an entire class of human beings, wash its hands of so profound a problem, and still live at peace with itself.

This is why, when the pundits were writing my political obituary, I dismissed it as nonsense. In Pennsylvania, we had passed the Abortion Control Act. It required such things as parental consent for minors, a twenty-four-hour waiting period, informed consent, and a ban on "sex-selection" abortions—meaning a child could not be aborted merely because he or she was not of the desired gender. Why were we able to pass that law? One very simple reason: By far the majority of Pennsylvanians agreed.

How many parents do not believe they have a right to know if their teenage daughter is about to place herself in the hands of an abortionist? How many people—in Pennsylvania, America, anywhere—believe that abortion is a proper recourse for parents disappointed to learn they will have a girl when they were hoping for a boy, or vice versa? You don't have to look at a poll to know that the American people oppose gender-selection abortions. Of course they do. The whole idea is monstrous—discarding babies of the "wrong" sex. Put the issue directly to people in a poll, and I guarantee that those against such abortions will be somewhere over 90 percent.

Leaving aside the Republicans, I would take the pro-life point even further. I believe that a qualified pro-life Democrat running for president cannot lose. Such a candidacy would have broad appeal. One of these days—soon, I hope—the national Democratic Party will wake up and discover that abortion on demand is not only morally wrong, it is also a long-term loser in political terms. I believe Republican national leaders know this. Millions of traditional national Democrats sit uneasily among the ranks of Republicans, driven there by a hostility among national Democratic leaders to their most deeply held principles. When Democratic leaders abandoned the unborn child, they abandoned the essence of the Democratic Party.

But in most other respects these millions of former Democrats are not quite at home in their new party, with its laissez-faire strain of social thinking. The "despotic individualism" driving the abortion cause, as Professor George McKenna put it in a 1995 *Atlantic Monthly* essay, belongs more to Republicans than Democrats: "If Democrats are pro-choice for political reasons, Republicans are pro-choice in their hearts." Here, he refers to the "Rockefeller Republicans" who have historically been liberal on the so-called "social issues," especially abortion.

This is actually borne out by the Reagan phenomenon. Politically, Ronald Reagan's great achievement was to expand the Republican base beyond the monied, well-to-do wing of the party represented by the "Rockefeller Republicans" to include middle-class working families who had historically been key elements of the Democratic coalition — the "Reagan Democrats."

The "Reagan Democrat," more often than not, is the pro-life Democrat. Reagan won by winning their allegiance. Without the Reagan Democrat, Republicans would be in serious trouble. How often have we heard these voters described as "holding the balance of power" in national elections? It is ludicrous to hear liberal Republicans urging a "Big Tent" on the abortion issue to make room for pro-choice Republicans. The moment Republicans surrender on the issue, they won't need any tent at all for the lawn-party-sized crowd that will linger after the exodus. A pup-tent would suffice. The real issue is money: the big donors tend to be pro-choice, and don't much care for the pro-life "element" they are always complaining about in the media. I believe such a position misreads and underestimates the power of the social revolution driving the national political dynamic in the country today.

A pro-life Democratic candidate for president, by contrast, would draw millions back into the ranks — more than enough to cover the loss in pro-abortion votes. I believe that, and that alone, is what prevents some Republican leaders from surrendering the abortion issue. There is nothing they fear more than the prospect of pro-life Democrats regaining control of their party, as they surely will in time.

But the deeper reason for my belief is this. From the very start, the abortion cause has depended upon silence. Any time the question is put directly to them — "Do you favor abortion on demand?" — by far the majority of Americans say no. But if you ask the same people what the law now permits, most will say it permits abortions only in the earlier stages of pregnancy.

In other words, most people do not know that under current law the abortion license is absolute — that, for example, 40 percent of abortions are *second* or even *third* abortions. In most places in America today, a woman can get an abortion for any reason at all.

Every so often in the abortion debate, the truth begins to slip out, as in the 1995 debate over "partial birth abortions." The details are appalling. When people hear of them, they're stunned. The abortion lobby then flies into action. Who will ever forget Rep. Patricia Schroeder, in the House debate over partial birth abortions, scolding pro-life Republicans and Democrats for dwelling on the "gruesome details."

Unfortunately, that is what the whole debate is about—little details like hands and feet and beating hearts. The entire pro-choice movement can best be described as a massive conspiracy of silence as to those "little details." Above all, the aim is to keep those details as far away from the minds of young women as possible.

A few years ago, for example, there was a film, in ultrasonic images, called *The Silent Scream*. It was produced by Dr. Bernard Nathanson, himself a former abortionist and founder of the National Abortion Rights Action League. It showed an unborn baby flinching—literally recoiling—from the abortionist's intrusion into the womb. It would take a very hard person to watch that film and not do some flinching. It is horrible to watch.

But why have we not seen this film on television? We hear enough about the right to choose: What about the right to information? After all, America's television and cable network executives and reporters are hardly known for their squeamishness. Day after day, we are confronted with images of the most graphic and brutal kind. When people are starving to death in faraway lands, those stark images are brought into every household in America—often with wonderful results. Our hearts are moved. Money is raised. Food and medical supplies are airlifted. The best in America is brought out. Why, on this one issue, have the networks never chosen to confront us with these startling images? No issue in America today is debated so exhaustively or heatedly as abortion. Yet somehow, uncharacteristically, the media spare us all the unpleasantness of having to see—even in ultrasonic images—the thing we are actually debating. I have always believed that if a film like *The Silent Scream* were shown one evening on network television, overnight the poll numbers would jump off the charts. A few more showings, and the abortion debate would be over.

In the same way, pro-choice advocates have always opposed laws such as Pennsylvania's simply requiring "informed consent," with the risks of the procedure carefully explained as in any other invasive procedure. Their answer is that informed consent only traumatizes a woman who is already undergoing terrible stress. The idea, they charge, is just a malicious attempt by pro-lifers to torment women who have chosen to have an abortion. In the case of Pennsylvania, this is a particularly hollow charge: We didn't offer uplifting lectures to women and then abandon mother and child to their fate. We surrounded them with services of every kind—public and private—to help.

But the criticism only begs the question: Why would anyone feel tormented by images of an unborn child? What don't they want the young woman to see? The inescapable answer is that what the young woman would see is—a baby.

For me, the most humbling experience in my eight years in office was to meet women who had seen through the big lie and brought their unborn babies to term. Some had had abortions before, but just couldn't bring themselves do it again. Some were raising children with absent fathers. For some it meant the choice of raising children while holding down a job. Others were raising a child with Down's Syndrome or some similar challenge. Still others heroically carried the child to term and placed the newborn for adoption.

They are people I felt privileged to *know*, privileged to represent in office. They are the quiet leaders in a social revolution far more powerful than any political lobby or faction. Each had passed through her own wall of fire, finding life on the other side.

In each case, the modern world stood ready with a wide range of available excuses, rationalizations, and routes of escape—all promising a higher "quality of life." But they didn't follow. Through all the shouting and marching and accusations, they heard another voice.

So long as there are such women, there is hope for every one of us— for people in all political parties, in all classes, of all faiths. That's why the whole abortion movement is in the end destined to pass away. It was doomed from the start. In the end, after all, there are no movements: There are just people—human beings left alone with their consciences.

Someone has described conscience as "the still point in the turning wheel." It remains so today in the abortion debate. Informed conscience, not intolerance, is the real enemy of the abortion industry. What are all the pro-choice slogans worth when we stop and look at a sonogram—that beautiful picture of life in the womb given to us by modern technology? Amid all the pro-choice rallies and marches and court arguments, there will always be that same silence, and in that silence we will always hear the same voice—the sound of a child crying out for life.

I will never forget a letter I received from a little girl in Hollsopple, Pennsylvania, a small town in Somerset County. When I packed up and left Harrisburg after my second term, it was among my most prized possessions:

> Dear Governor Casey:
>
> Hi! My name is Jessica Stobaugh. I am ten. I was adopted. My birth mom chose life for me. I would stand up like you for life. I think what you are doing is right. I would do the same thing if I were the governor. I am proud to live in Pennsylvania because you are the governor of our state. Thank you for fighting for unborn children, even when it's a hard thing to do.
>
> From your fan and friend,
> Jessica

That letter, in all its beautiful simplicity, has been a continuing source of inspiration and encouragement in the long struggle to protect the unborn child.

My foe in 1990 when I ran for reelection was Pennsylvania Auditor General Barbara Hafer, a pro-choice Republican. Somebody must have thought she had a chance to become governor—she raised some two million dollars for her campaign. A Democratic pollster named Harrison Hickman claimed to have a poll showing that, once my pro-life position became known, the election would be a virtual dead heat. One of Hafer's supporters, the Pittsburgh representative of the National Organization for Women, was even more optimistic, predicting that "Casey will be dead by November." I'm still not sure if this was her electoral or medical prognosis.

In any case, I enlisted my old campaign team from '86—James Carville, Bob Shrum, David Doak, and Mike Donilon—and together we made our case to the people. Throughout the campaign, reporters stressed that abortion was the driving issue behind the Hafer candidacy, until I won by a million votes—whereupon they reported with a yawn that "abortion was not an issue." It was a classic example of our modern media at work, tailoring the news to suit their own prejudices. Carville didn't let them get away with it. His post-election comment said it all: "If Bob Casey was a pro-choice Episcopalian, he'd be on the cover of *Time* magazine."

Two vivid memories of the '90 campaign stay with me. The first occurred one afternoon when I looked out the window of the govenor's residence to find a group of pro-abortion activists marching outside the gate, shouting, "Get your rosaries off my ovaries!" It was a snapshot of the whole abortion debate: Soon after the local news crew had packed up the cameras and departed, the handful of protesters threw their placards in their cars and sped off. And that was that. The end of a day's work.

The other incident came after Ms. Hafer's description of me, in a Philadelphia speech, as that "rednecked Irishman from Scranton." She should have run the phrase by her pollster first, because just about everybody in both parties was offended. Compounding matters, she refused to apologize.

Soon afterward I attended the St. Patrick's Day Parade in Philadelphia—a day I doubt she was looking forward to. The parade committee had invited me as governor and invited Ms. Hafer as the state's auditor general. But when I arrived, one of the organizers said to me, "We had to withdraw the invitation to Barbara Hafer. We told her we couldn't guarantee her safety." Ms. Hafer took this advice and skipped the happy occasion.

I'll never forget sitting in the reviewing stand and watching the parade delegations from the building trades march by, hundreds of them, all with bright red ribbons around their collars, looking up and giving me the "thumbs up" sign of support.

When the votes were counted, I'd received 68 percent of the total. It was a landslide win of over a million votes, the largest margin in Pennsylvania gubernatorial history. We carried sixty-six of sixty-seven counties, losing narrowly in Montgomery County. We could see it coming in places like Lancaster County, a county no Democrat had ever before carried. I carried it by more than forty thousand votes for one simple reason: For Republicans and Democrats, the cause of protecting children is bigger than either party.

14

An Upset Landslide

The 1992 presidential election began the night Harris Wofford was elected.

ONE OF THE saddest events of my years as governor occurred April 4, 1991, when United States Senator John Heinz was killed in a plane crash near Philadelphia. The state was plunged into mourning. Senator Heinz was very popular—and more importantly, respected.

Ellen and I felt the loss personally. We knew John Heinz. We liked and admired him; we respected him. Just a short time before his death we sat next to him in Greensburg, Pennsylvania, at a church service for the young service men and women who had been killed in a Scud missile attack during the final days of the Persian Gulf War. He was still in his forties, a strong, confident, and imposing figure of a man. I remember him talking with great pride that day about his children and what they were doing. John Heinz had everything to live for. Now, suddenly and inexplicably, he was gone.

The task of filling the Senate vacancy caused by his death fell to me as governor. Talk was already placing former Governor Dick Thornburgh, President Bush's attorney general, as the sure Republican candidate in the coming race for the vacant seat.

My task was to appoint someone highly qualified, and also strong enough to run for the full term in the election that would follow. Congressman John Murtha suggested Lee Iacocca. Murtha had just invited Iacocca to speak in Johnstown. On paper, it seemed a good idea. He was a graduate of Lehigh University, a native of Allentown, Pennsylvania, and his mother still lived there. Of course, he lived in Michigan since he was chairman of Chrysler Corporation. At the time, he had a compelling personal story as a successful business executive and could raise the necessary financial support to mount a campaign. "Why not go and at least talk to him?" Murtha suggested.

Iacocca was intrigued by the idea at first, but then asked not to be considered. The press found out about it, and made light of the fact that I would even entertain such a notion. I just saw it as a possibility worth exploring.

The appointment process thrust upon me was just one more political problem I didn't need. Finally, I selected Harris Wofford. We had been friends since the 1950s when we were associates at the firm of Covington & Burling in Washington. At my urging, he had served as Pennsylvania Democratic state chairman during my campaign for governor in 1986. He had been President Kennedy's special assistant for civil rights, an early leader of the Peace Corps under Sargent Shriver, and a president of Bryn Mawr College. After my election, I had appointed him secretary of the Department of Labor and Industry in my cabinet. He also supported Pennsylvania's Abortion Control Act. No one gave him a chance to beat Thornburgh in an election, but most agreed he was a strong choice.

We would change that perception of Wofford's election prospects. What we didn't know was just how dramatically we would change it, and what effect his victory would have on the next national election.

Once again my entire campaign team came on board for Wofford's campaign: James Carville, Paul Begala, Bob Shrum, David Doak, Mike Donilon.

Thornburgh announced for the race, and the instant consensus was that he was a sure thing. To my surprise, though, Thornburgh seriously misread the public mood in Pennsylvania by announcing he'd "walked the corridors of power" in Washington. That was the last thing Pennsylvania voters wanted to hear. There was already a deepening disenchantment with the Bush administration.

Meanwhile, our candidate, Wofford, was having difficulty raising money while we'd heard that the Republican senatorial campaign committee intended to fund the Thornburgh campaign very generously. Once again, everything would come down to fund-raising. I knew Wofford had no chance without the money to run a competitive race. So we set up a meeting with Senate Majority Leader George Mitchell to try to pry some money loose from the Democratic senatorial campaign committee. I well knew that the Washington Democratic establishment seldom offered money to help long shots.

The Wofford campaign had taken a poll by Mike Donilon, and the poll turned up something very interesting. The opening question simply asked which candidate the voter would support: Thornburgh, the Republican, or Wofford, the Democrat. Thornburgh came out ahead by almost fifty points. A complete wipeout. No chance.

But then there was question number six in the poll, and it changed everything. It described Thornburgh's experience and career as governor and attorney general in very positive terms, and then went on to describe Wofford's background and experience. It specifically mentioned Wofford's being in favor of health insurance for American families. After that, the poll asked, "Now, having the benefit of that information on both candidates, if the election for the United States Senate were held today and the candidates were Dick Thornburgh, the Republican, and Harris Wofford, the Democrat, for whom would you vote?"

Amazingly, the voters now chose Wofford over Thornburgh by five percentage points! We knew from that one question that Wofford had more than just a chance. He could win. Mike Donilon said he had never seen such a turnaround in all his experience with polls.

I knew we were going before a group of party potentates who were strapped for campaign funds, and were convinced from media reports that Wofford was doomed. The meeting was held in the office of Senator Mitchell. I had talked with him on the phone several times during the appointment process and also after Wofford's selection. I'd made it clear to Mitchell that I had just come through my own re-election campaign for which we still had debts to pay. I told him that I would do what I could to support the Wofford campaign financially, but that I could not do it alone because of my own campaign debt.

The meeting was delayed because of the late arrival of some of the senators. Senator Charles Robb, chairman of the senatorial campaign committee, was there, along with Senators Rockefeller, Breaux, and Bryan. Wofford and Paul Begala were with me for the meeting. The senators were in a hurry. Senator Robb wasted no time in pleading penury: The committee simply did not have that much money, and had to invest its limited funds with care. Senator Mitchell was even more pre-emptory. He turned to me and said, "Governor, you have three minutes to make your case."

"I know you all think that Thornburgh is invincible," I began. "You've been reading all that Inside-the-Beltway stuff in the papers. Well, let me tell you something about Pennsylvania. This election is in Pennsylvania, not inside the Beltway. And in Pennsylvania, Governor Thornburgh has never faced an opponent with a first-class, experienced campaign team that knows how to use television and knows how to win. Wofford will have that going for him. Thornburgh just might have a glass jaw."

Then I read them question number six from the poll.

"I'm telling you right now that Wofford can win if we give him the financial support he needs."

Mitchell interrupted, challenging me. "You're asking us to contribute to Wofford and yet you're raising money for your own campaign committee. What are you going to do in Pennsylvania?"

"Wait a minute, Senator; I told you from the beginning that I had to complete payment on my campaign obligations. You knew that from day one. We will do our part in Pennsylvania. The question I am putting to you today is this: Do you want to win this seat or don't you? If you do, then Wofford needs a million dollars, and he needs it now. Do you want a Democratic senator from Pennsylvania, or don't you?"

They did. They contributed nine hundred twenty thousand dollars to the Wofford campaign, and he was off and running.

Thornburgh's campaign strategy quickly became clear. He decided to make me the issue, since I had appointed Wofford, and had just made massive budget cuts followed by a big tax increase. He launched a television blitz featuring a grainy picture of Wofford and me on the day I appointed him. Thornburgh was banking on the hope that the tax increase I had just signed would sink Wofford.

It was a phony issue: Wofford had already left my cabinet at the time the tax legislation went through. But Thornburgh nevertheless spent a fortune on television attacking me in order to defeat Wofford. He got my attention. I decided to accept the challenge.

For the next few months, through the winter and early spring of 1991, I'd leave my office in the capitol at every opportunity and go to the office of the Real Bob Casey Committee—still opened for business to retire our campaign debts—to make fund-raising phone calls for Wofford. My message was simple: "Harris Wofford is going to win, and I can prove it. Let me read you this poll." And I would read them question number six. The money came pouring in.

While Thornburgh was reminding voters he had walked the corridors of power, Wofford put the healthcare issue front and center. He ran a strong campaign and proved to be an excellent candidate. The result was that Attorney General Thornburgh became the focus of all the voter dissatisfaction with the Bush administration; his strategy of connecting himself with the Washington power structure worked exactly in reverse. Wofford got the benefit of the backlash against President Bush.

On election night, he achieved that rare political feat described by Carville as "an upset landslide." Wofford began the campaign forty-seven points behind in the polls; he won with a ten-point margin, by over three hundred-fifty thousand votes. It was a political shot heard round the world. The Republican and Democratic political establishments were rocked by the news.

The 1992 presidential election began the night Harris Wofford was elected. This Pennsylvania Senate race was the beginning of the end for the Bush administration: If a political novice could win in an upset landslide against President Bush's attorney general, who was also a former governor of the state, what did this say about Bush's re-election prospects? I received a phone call not long after that election from Arkansas Governor Bill Clinton. Would I call James Carville and urge him to manage the Clinton presidential campaign? As it turned out, I didn't have to. Carville called me first. He had decided to cast his lot with Clinton.

15

My Foes

At that moment, none of our differences through the years meant a thing.

"YOU NEED to get out of here," Dr. Starzl was saying. "Why don't you go back to Harrisburg and take back your powers as governor?"

It had been less than two weeks since my surgery, and already Dr. Starzl was prodding me to get moving, as if I were just some loafer living the life of Riley in my hospital suite. But I knew what he was up to. "You need to get out of here," he continued. "Hospitals are full of germs. Besides, they want to regiment your entire life, from the time you wake up 'til the time you close your eyes at night."

It was his way of saying, "Okay, time to get up and live again." But while I understood this psychological strategy, I also felt like a giant pin cushion not quite ready yet to re-assume the duties of governor.

During these pep talks of Dr. Starzl's, I would look helplessly down at the intravenous needles and tubes binding me to the bed. "Do you really think it's time?" I'd ask, hoping the poignancy of this sight would hold Starzl at bay.

Along with the tubes and wires, there was the further problem of profound fatigue. For days, I hadn't been able to eat a thing, despite orders to put on weight. Matt was bringing me extra food from the cafeteria, yet even that wasn't making a dent. I was miserable, and a little wary of the doctor's cheery stratagems.

This ritual went on for a week until one day Starzl came in and announced we were all going on a picnic the following Saturday.

"Picnic!" Ellen gasped. "He'll never be able to go to a picnic!"

When the day arrived and I grumbled something about not even having "the right clothes" for the outing, Starzl held up a jacket, saying, "Here, let's go."

"What does Dr. Fung think about this?" I countered, certain that in him I would find an ally. Dr. Fung was brought in, dutifully read his lines—"I think it is a very good idea"—departed, and with that the question was settled. Within minutes I was out of bed, dressed, and walking through the front door of the hospital.

Even the state troopers could not stand in Dr. Starzl's way. "The governor will have to ride in the state car," explained one.

"He's coming with me," replied the doctor.

In a compromise, a trooper was stuffed into the backseat of Starzl's car. With the doctor, his wife Joy, Ellen and me packed in, off we went. Soon all doubts vanished. Driving along in the sun and the wind and the fresh air, I felt like a new man.

The picnic, a staff outing arranged by the medical center, was held at a park in O'Hara Township. When we arrived and I got out of the car, dozens of people who had been milling around stopped in their tracks, as if seeing an apparition. In what I still count as one of the nicest moments of my life, they all smiled and applauded as I walked toward them.

For an hour I sat in the sun, chatting with doctors and nurses and passersby. Doctors had come from all over the world to study with Dr. Starzl. Many of the people involved with saving my life were there, too, and one of them reached over and plopped a straw hat on my head— one of those Caribbean-style, wide-brim deals. I'm glad no camera crew was around to preserve the image for posterity, but at the moment it felt perfect and I wore my big straw hat proudly.

Not a week later, Dr. Starzl was back in my room. Another outing. "You know," he said, "I'm supposed to throw out the first ball tonight at the Pirates game at Three Rivers Stadium. Why don't you do it for me?"

Sure, I was doing better, and the picnic had done wonders. But that particular day had not been a good one. I felt very weak.

"Doctor," I felt like saying, "from this very bed I'll wager I could throw a straighter pitch than you will tonight. But no, I think I'll leave the honor to you. You've earned it. I'll be watching on TV—good luck."

Instead I just said I'd take a raincheck; I didn't feel up to it.

"Okay," he replied, "but it sure would be a big surprise for everybody if you showed up."

With that, he left. Sure enough, I got to thinking about the satisfaction of strolling into Three Rivers Stadium, waving a cap to the fans. Much of my life had centered around sports. At one point, I'd even had a shot at the Philadelphia Phillies farm team. My sons and I had shared some of our best moments at the ballpark. Soon the idea to attend the game took hold of me, and I decided to suit up.

Putting on my Pirates cap that night as I left with Ellen, I felt like Jimmy Stewart in *The Monty Stratton Story*. It had been a long layoff. They said I'd never pitch again. But here I was.

As it turned out, however, throwing out the first ball would have to wait. It was hard enough just to get to Three Rivers, so I had to content myself with watching the game from an upper-level box. Dr. Starzl did the pitching.

"How are you feeling?" reporters asked as we entered the stadium. "When are you coming back?"

I pointed to my cap, which said: "Pittsburgh, All-Star City, 1994 All-Star Game." The All-Star Game was planned for the next year, 1994. I told them, "My goal is to be back one year from now. And I'm telling you that's exactly what I intend to do."

Dr. Starzl and his wife, Joy, were in the box that night, sitting one row down in front of us. As I looked at him I had to smile. A few hours earlier I was in a hospital bed feeling sorry for myself, and now here I was living again. What an amazing person he was.

"I hate hospitals!" he'd told me. I had even heard that Dr. Starzl

[165]

himself had had a heart attack on the way to work. He staggered up the steps to his office, lay on the floor until the pain passed, got up, and worked until nearly midnight. Several days later, he took a flight to San Francisco for a medical meeting, holding forth at the meeting, and then checked himself into the hospital for open-heart surgery. Three days later, he pulled out the I.V. tubes from his own arm and left the hospital.

I'd heard such stories, and now I knew they were all true. Tom Starzl was a fighter. When it came to innovative surgical techniques to save lives, he was daring and brash: the James Carville of the operating suite. But he believed in others as much as he believed in himself. Being with him was like getting a daily transfusion of courage. "You're in for the fight of your life, Governor, but you are going to win." When he had said that before the operation, it wasn't a prediction—it was a direct order. He hadn't just led or inspired me through that wall of fire, he had commanded me.

And there he was that night sitting in front of me, absorbed in the ballgame, rarely even looking back to check on his patient. That would have suggested worry. His patient would be just fine. Starzl was the picture of confidence. On an impulse I took off my cap, reached over, and placed it on his head.

The day finally came to leave the hospital. On July 27, I went home. I guess it's one of the defense mechanisms we all have within us to block out and not remember each little detail of sickness or suffering. It is a good thing humans were made that way, so we wouldn't waste time dwelling on all the specifics of our own plight. The period following the transplant covered a timespan of about six weeks. My most vivid memory is of seemingly never-ending bouts with needles and tubes—I.V. tubes constantly being inserted in arms and, later, near the collarbone—and the train of nurses, doctors, and surgeons coming and going. Several times a day a team of people would come in and pound on my back and sides for fifteen minutes or so. The purpose of this unsettling ritual was to break loose and cause me to cough up thick congealed blood from my lungs. The stuff looked like motor oil. But I had to get it out of my system.

And every day, all day, and after dinner at night, Ellen and Matt were there with me. Sitting with me in my room. Bringing in food so I could gain weight. Helping me in endless ways, large and small, every day. I would never have come through without them. My young son, in those hard and painful months, was almost parental in the solicitude and strength he showered upon me.

During that critical time, there had been a general outpouring of prayers, support, and good wishes that I would not have thought possible. When I left intensive care and could read some of the mail, I was amazed to find that one of the very first letters I had received was from former President Ronald Reagan. With it was a message from Governor Thornburgh. It had come the very morning of my surgery. There were letters, calls, and telegrams by the hundreds from all over Pennsylvania, all over the country. President Clinton had called several times, once from Philadelphia on the Fourth of July. He was there to take part in the award of the Medal of Freedom at Independence Hall to Vaclev Havel. From all around, I was buoyed up by the love and support of thousands of well-wishers, most of them strangers.

Each time I seemed to be in trouble, the entire team of doctors rallied to my side: Starzl; Fung; Tzakis; Follansbee; Dr. Toby Graham; Dr. Shimon Kusne, an infectious disease specialist; my transplant coordinator Bridget Flynn; and so many others.

I had to fight off two serious viruses that Michael Lucas's heart and liver had carried. They landed me back in the hospital later that fall and on heavy virus-killing drugs for quite a while afterwards. Late one afternoon I began to fill chilled. Blankets were brought in, but it made no difference. I just kept getting colder. I began to shudder and shake uncontrollably. Then my temperature shot up. Ellen wasn't there. She had gone to Scranton to attend a shower for Pat's fiancée, Anne Cannon. It was the only day she was away from me the whole time, and I had insisted on her going.

The spiking fever was like a mayday alert. Infection, I knew, was one of the twin threats to transplant patients. The other, of course, was rejection. I went from feeling frozen to burning up with a high fever. And this went on into the night. I kept coming in and out of consciousness. Things were not good, and the doctors stayed close by. I remember waking up around 4:00 A.M. There was Dr. Follansbee looking down on me. And then—inexplicably, it seemed—the fever left me.

Just about every day for months after the surgery, Dr. Andreas Tzakis came to see me, especially when I was suffering from the viral infections which sent me back in the hospital in the fall of 1993. His own story is an inspiration. Though now recognized as an expert in his field, he was told early in his career that he lacked the requisite dexterity to become a transplant surgeon. Undaunted, he refused to accept rejection, and for the next several years carried surgical instruments around with him wherever he went until they became almost a natural extension of his hands. He then renewed his request to perform transplants, and was accepted.

Today Dr. Tzakis specializes in liver transplants. Many of his cases involve children. During my recuperation Andy performed an extraordinary operation on a child from England. The child had undergone a prior transplant of a stomach organ which his body had rejected. He became deathly ill and, as a last resort, the decision was made to conduct a transplant of seven other stomach organs. I believe it may have been the first time such a procedure was attempted. The boy survived for several weeks, but passed away. I remember how deeply the child's death affected Andy.

I remember his telling me a happier story about another child who survived. The child lived on an Indian reservation in the western United States, and Andy accompanied his patient back home. He stayed with his patient and described vividly the religious ceremony conducted by the tribe to welcome the child back into the tribe. Dr. Tzakis is now director of the transplant program at the University of Miami in Florida. I can never thank him enough.

As I was waiting for my own transplant surgery to begin, a doctor came to my room to explain the anesthesiology to be administered. His name was Leonard Firestone. It was late Sunday night, June 13. "I was out in my garden this afternoon," he said, "when I got a phone call telling me to report back to the hospital for surgery. Frankly, I wasn't too happy to have my weekend interrupted. But then I came in and looked at your chart and the data which have been compiled on you. I just want you to know that I feel very good about this. You're in excellent condition for this procedure, and I believe you'll come through it just fine."

I can't tell you what a great lift those few words from Dr. Firestone gave me. The surgery was drawing closer and I had been left alone with my thoughts and fears. Later I learned that Dr. Firestone was among the leading anesthesiologists in the country and the author of books on the subject. There's that luck again. I will always be grateful for his skill, and for the confidence he gave me at a crucial hour.

Listening to my story, you would think all my doctors were brash and visionary men. Not so. Few were as helpful to me as Dr. Toby Graham. She is a gastroenterologist. Because amyloid affects the gastrointestinal system, Toby worked with me day after day with my diet, medications, and supplemental nutrition, among many other things.

She and Dr. Follansbee advocated the use of the Hickman catheter to give me supplemental nutrition after I had returned to Harrisburg. The surgeons—particularly Dr. Starzl and Dr. Tzakis—were opposed to the idea because anytime plastic tubes are inserted into a patient, there's always the danger of infection. The doctors openly debated the pros and cons of the catheter—right in front of me—and finally a compromise was struck. I would use the catheter on a trial basis and the doctors would closely monitor the progress to guard against infection.

The downside, from my standpoint, was that a new surgical incision would be made in my chest and a tube inserted. I was given hyperalimentation through that tube every night, while I slept. It was really an I.V. tube directly into the chest rather than through a vein in my arm. The hyperalimentation was in a large plastic container. It was white and looked like liquefied flour. It hung from an I.V. pole at my bed, and Ellen and Matt (who had postponed law school a year to stay by my side) became experts on how to work the pump on the I.V. pole which pushed the liquid into my body. Often in the middle of the night, they would hear the pump beeping, which meant the line was blocked or otherwise malfunctioning. One or the other—or both—would get up and fix the line. This treatment went on for months and really got me "over the hump," giving me the extra nourishment my body needed in order to heal. There were no problems with infection.

Follow-up care is always important after surgery, but even more so after a transplant. In my case, the job fell to Bridget Flynn, my nurse and transplant coordinator. She worked with me, day after day, through all the ups and downs of recovery, from intensive care right up to the present moment. She was my counselor on medical matters, and quickly became a family friend whom Ellen and I like and admire enormously.

We have also become friends, especially Matt, with Dr. Rod Stephenson, a young transplant surgeon and regular on the post-transplant team of physicians who cared for me. During that night of high fever and bone-rattling chills, he was there. Rod received his prior training at Meharry Medical College in Nashville and has returned there to continue his career in Tennessee.

And through it all, from May 1993 through the surgery and recovery—to this very day—Dr. John Fung has been the mainstay of my medical team. I literally owe him my life. He is not only a world-class surgeon, but he and his family have become our good friends.

Part of what kept me going after the surgery, I must admit, was a sheer desire to put a lot of doubters in their place. From the moment they heard of my illness, long before my surgery, the oddsmakers in Harrisburg were convinced I was through. Then, when my intention to undergo transplantation was made public, the oddsmakers doubted I would survive the risky surgery. When I survived, they began to make book on my early political retirement. It may not speak particularly well of me, it may not be the noblest motive, but I *lived* for the day when I would walk into the Capitol, see the stunned looks on their faces (especially the reporters) and say, "Okay, what's all the commotion? Everybody get back to work!"

I count many friends among the media. But there were a few stories circulating about my surgery that seemed eager to emphasize the

"Casey-to-Step-Down" angle. Out of sheer competitive pride, I relished the opportunity to write my own storyline. Asked by the scribes what my plans were, I said: "As sure as the sun will come up tomorrow, I'll be back to finish my second term. Bet the house on it."

In a way, though, we were all proved wrong. On the day of my return to the Capitol, December 21, 1993—six months and a week after the surgery—there were no foes to greet me, no stunned looks, no disappointed rivals. Everybody was happy. All pettiness, including my own, fell away in a general atmosphere of rejoicing.

I had reclaimed my powers as governor at 12:01 A.M. that morning. A ceremony was set for later in the day to make it official. When it began, I stood for a moment at the bottom of the steps of the entrance to the capitol, drinking it all in. I remember the crush of reporters and television cameras at the top of the steps as I climbed them one by one, unable to see their faces in the blinding lights, but behind them were the jubilant roaring, whistling, clapping, shouted messages of welcome. The sound was deafening. A banner stretched across the capitol corridor, which read: "Welcome Back, Governor. Your return is our best Christmas present!"

I stepped up to the microphone. It was all too much. I didn't know what to do, how to begin, and I said so.

When I found my voice, I said, "By the grace of God, a loving family, the skill of my doctors, and the support of our people, I am here today. I have come to believe that if you want something badly enough, and are willing to work hard to achieve it, nothing is impossible. If we work together, nothing can stop us.

"I was re-elected in 1990 by the people of this state to serve a four-year term and that, with the help of God and the people of Pennsylvania, is what I intend to try to do. I came back because it was my duty to come back. A lot of people are hurting today, and we've got to help them. That's what I came back to do."

Standing up there as I spoke, I saw something I will never, ever forget. In the front row sat three of my colleagues in the trenches: Lieutenant Governor Mark Singel, who had been serving as acting governor; Senate Democratic Leader J. William Lincoln; and my longtime political foe, Senate Republican Leader Robert Jubelirer. They were weeping openly. If they were my own brothers they could not have been more happy for me. We were "two old political enemies," Senator Jubelirer told reporters that day, "but that doesn't mean a thing when it comes to people's lives and families. To see the miracle of Bob Casey is one of the most heart-rending moments of my life. To see him come back from the dead—I tell you, isn't this a great country?"

I felt the exactly the same way. At that moment, none of our differences through the years meant a thing. I had walked through the valley of death; I had come back; here were my friends to greet me; praise the Lord!

It was a beautiful ceremony. Ten days later something happened which made me feel that I was really in command again. A brutal winter storm hit the region. That New Year's Eve was one of the coldest in memory. As everyone was about to take off for the holiday, I was told the money that provided heating oil to low-income families was running out. Unless something was done, a lot of people would go without heat.

I hate to sound like the hero of every story, but frankly I felt really good at that moment. In a way, I needed the use of power as much as those people needed warmth. And it was not, after all, a complicated problem. I picked up the phone, called Chief of Staff Jim Brown, and instructed him to order the Department of Public Welfare to make more money available immediately. He in turn called the deputy director of the department, caught her as she was on her way to a New Year's Eve celebration, and told her to get it done.

That's what I'd always liked best about being governor. When problems occured, I didn't call a task force to ponder it and report back in six months. I didn't pound the desk and say, "People are shivering in freezing-cold apartments—let's run this by our focus group!" I could pick up the phone and say, "Do this—right now. End of discussion." I wasn't always that firm, but I like to think in my best moments I used my power as it was meant to be used—decisively and in defense of the powerless.

You would think that under the circumstances of my return to office—the last year of my final term after recovering from a major operation, with a still-divided legislature—I would be the lamest of lame ducks. In fact, that final year was a pretty successful one, with a few rough spots and hard calls along the way.

The steepest hill every year is the budget. Once that is behind, a major part of the year's work is done. In 1995 we got it done early. Only the second time that happened in my two terms in office. It was even more remarkable because I was faced with a split among fellow Democrats in the House, arising from my proposal in the budget to cut business taxes and impose a work requirement on our able-bodied general-assistance recipients. But the budget passed the House overwhelmingly, with about half the Democratic votes and all the Republican votes. And we had similar good luck in the Senate. We also cut the personal income tax for poor and working families by substantially increasing the deduction for children. And we produced a surplus of five hundred million dollars after the budget was balanced, and completed reform of our workers' compensation law to lower business costs without hurting workers.

That was the political high-point. The low points came in three decisions I made that year.

The first of these was the Reginald McFadden case. In March 1994, several months after my return to work, I had to decide the fate of McFadden, who was serving a life sentence in state prison. He had been in prison from the time he was sixteen until the age of forty. He had received a strong recommendation from the Pardons Board to commute his life sentence with only the attorney general dissenting. Based on the record presented to me, I concluded that Reginald McFadden had been rehabilitated. I granted the commutation.

Late one afternoon in October, I received a call from Jim Brown, my chief of staff. Also on the line was Vince Carocci, my press secretary. The Associated Press had called them about a wire story out of New York, reporting McFadden's arrest for the rape and robbery of a New York woman. He was also a suspect in the death of another woman and a man in New York. The AP was asking for comment. I issued a statement taking full responsibility for the decision to commute McFadden's sentence and called for his punishment to the full extent of the law if found guilty of the offenses charged against him.

Eventually, McFadden was convicted of the rape and robbery of the woman, and pleaded guilty to one of the murder charges. Nothing I could say then or now would change anything. Nor is there any solace in the fact that, of the one hundred-thirty-seven recommendations for commutation in my eight years as governor, I turned down one hundred-twelve and granted only twenty-five—and only in this case was I proved wrong. Of those I granted, several prisoners were terminally ill. To my knowledge, all the others went on to lead lawful lives. But none of this eases the sorrow, least of all for McFadden's victims and their families, or the deep personal pain I feel. I was later in New York City to receive the Cardinal Cooke pro-life award, and was encircled by TV cameras and reporters asking me how I could represent myself as a champion of life when I had contributed to this brutality against innocent people. I felt it was more complicated than that, but I accepted full responsibility. The decision to commute was my decision; it was my signature on the release papers; and I alone bore responsibility for the commutation. I can only hope that the victims and their families will find it in their hearts to forgive me for the grievous results of that decision.

The McFadden case had political consequences, too, in the 1994 gubernatorial election. The story hit just twenty-five days before the November 8 election. The Democratic nominee was Lieutenant Governor Mark Singel, who had served faithfully and well as acting governor during my recovery. As a member of the Pardons Board, Singel had voted in favor of commuting McFadden's sentence. The Republican nominee, Congressman Tom Ridge, went on the attack with devastating effect.

The second decision involved my lieutenant governor, Mark Singel.

It was not an easy thing, but I had to decide not to campaign actively for Singel, whom I regarded not only as an ally but a friend. In the 1994 campaign, he decided to hedge on the pro-life principles I thought we shared, and which had formed an important part of our public record together. In private I had made it clear that I could not help him if he did so. Singel had, after all, been pro-life during our first term in office together, and those convictions had been my principal reason for selecting him in 1986. After our re-election in 1990, he decided, without my support, to run for United States Senate, and changed from pro-life to pro-choice. He went so far as to repudiate Pennsylvania's Abortion Control Act, one of the most notable accomplishments of our first term.

I regarded it at the time as a fatal political mistake, as well as a flip-flop on the merits of the issue. As a practical matter, he'd abandoned his pro-life constituency and never gained any pro-choice votes because he was still suspect in his new pro-choice camp. His primary opponent, Lynn Yeakel, favored abortion-on-demand. In 1992, Singel had lost the senatorial primary. I deeply regretted having to stand back when he ran for governor in 1994, but whether he had acted from expediency or a sincere philosophical conversion, I could not in good conscience actively campaign for him. I regarded his position on the abortion issue as a repudiation of the record we had compiled together, a repudiation I simply could not support.

The third decision involved the re-election campaign of Senator Wofford.

Wofford, for his part, had announced at a press conference the day I appointed him to the Senate that he supported the Pennsyvania Abortion Control Act. But when he got to Washington he, too, seemed to have a change of heart. He voted, for example, to advance the Freedom of Choice Act on the Senate calendar (by sending it from committee to the Senate floor) even though that law would have repealed Pennsylvania's Abortion Control Act. And he had cast other votes causing one to doubt his allegiance to the pro-life cause.

The break between us came on President Clinton's healthcare bill in 1994. With some reservation about the complexity of the plan, I had been a supporter of universal healthcare at the federal level, as well as in Pennsylvania. But my support for the plan ended when the Clinton administration included "abortion services" in the basic benefits package of their healthcare plan. The effect would be to make taxpayers pay, not only for the abortion procedure, but also the facilities which would guarantee "access" to abortions for all women. This would have created a newly expanded abortion industry overnight, backed by the federal treasury—just as the nursing-home industry mushroomed when the federal government began subsidizing nursing home services. It's one of the lesser known points in the abortion debate that in some 85 percent of counties in America, there are no abortion clinics—for the simple reason that the majority of people in those counties do not want them. The Clinton healthcare plan, I felt certain, would nationalize and subsidize the abortion industry, building new abortion clinics in areas of the country which did not have them, and increase dramatically the number of abortions performed everywhere.

Wofford and I had a private meeting in my office. He was a member of the Senate Finance Committee, which was considering the Clinton plan. Senator Dan Coats of Indiana was to offer an amendment in the committee to remove abortion from the basic benefits package. I urged Harris to vote for the Coats amendment, explaining how I believed the healthcare plan, with abortion in the basic benefits package, subverted the principles we shared. But he did not agree with my interpretation of the healthcare plan. His rebuttal to my arguments, however, left me unconvinced, and I told him that if he should follow his current course, he would have to do so without me. We shook hands, wished each other well, and he returned to Washington. Several days later, Senator Wofford voted against the Coats amendment. When he sought re-election in 1994, I still wished him well but found myself unable to actively campaign for him.

My decision had been wrenching: Harris and his lovely wife, Clare, were old friends. I liked and admired him. He had been a hard-working and effective member of my cabinet. And it was I who had appointed him to the Senate.

As it turned out, Harris lost by some two hundred thousand votes. If his reasons for his position on the abortion issue were practical, then he miscalculated: The loss of pro-life voters could well have cost him the election.

16

Circle of Friends

*If we were truly the party of "tolerance" and "inclusion," as
the convention speakers claimed—just a great big circle of
friends—what was the problem?*

ABOUT A YEAR before my operation, I found myself at Madison
Square Garden in New York City for the Democratic National
Convention.

In a sense my journey there had actually begun years earlier,
climaxing a few months before the convention in Washington at the
United States Supreme Court. When I arrived at the convention in July
1992, I was no longer just Governor Robert P. Casey from Pennsylvania;
I was the defendant in *Planned Parenthood of Southeastern Pennsylvania* v. *Casey*.

Not to put too fine a point on it, in party circles that case had made
me a marked man. While *Roe* v. *Wade*, the 1973 case that legalized
abortion, had been left standing, the Supreme Court in *Casey* had
upheld Pennsylvania's Abortion Control Act, which I had signed into
law. The case, for me, had been the result of twenty-five years' experience with the abortion issue, beginning in 1966—seven years before
Roe v. *Wade*.

The occasion was my first Democratic primary against Milton Shapp. New York had just passed a very liberal abortion law, and the question was, Would I sign such a law in Pennsylvania if it were to pass? Shapp's answer was that this was an issue only women fully understood: that he would appoint a women's commission to study the issue, if elected; and that he would sign such a law, if enacted, in Pennsylvania. My response was simple and unequivocal: If the law were to pass, I would veto it.

I am fairly certain that my position hurt me, because in a Democratic primary where turnout was historically relatively low, liberal voters turned out in disproportionately large numbers and thus exercised a disproportionate influence on the outcome.

But I took that position instinctively. The Catholic Church made it clear that it took no position in the primary. And many Catholics worked openly and actively for my opponent.

For me, the imperative of protecting unborn human life has always been a self-evident proposition. I cannot recall the subject of abortion ever being mentioned, much less discussed in depth, in school or at home. My position was simply a part of me from the very beginning.

When I was elected in 1986, both my Democratic opponent in the primary and Republican opponent in the general election were pro-choice. When Lieutenant Governor Scranton and I debated on statewide television, the inevitable question was asked: "If the Supreme Court overruled *Roe* v. *Wade*, and the Pennsylvania legislature passed a bill banning all abortion except to save the life of the mother, would you sign it?" Scranton said that, while there were "too many abortions" in our country, and we should work to reduce that number, he would veto the law banning abortion. My answer was, "Yes, I would sign such a law."

My campaign people thought that my answer, not couched in the usual qualifiers—no "ifs," no "ands," and no "buts"—would cost us the election.

But after I became governor, I came face-to-face for the first time with a conflict between my personal and public position on abortion, and what I regarded as the duty imposed by my oath of office to "sup-

port, obey, and defend" the Constitution of the United States. As a lawyer, I was trained to believe that the Constitution meant what the
United States Supreme Court said it meant. The consequence of that
line of reasoning was that I could not sign a law which was, on its face,
in direct conflict with what the Supreme Court had decided, even
when I did not agree with the Court's ruling.

The issue was squarely presented when our legislature, in December
1987, and before the *Webster* ruling, passed an abortion control law
which required a woman seeking an abortion to notify the father of the
child. This meant notifying the biological father, whether or not he was
the spouse of the woman. The Supreme Court had already struck down
as unconstitutional a spousal notification requirement in another case,
where the biological father was the woman's husband and the two were
living together in a normal domestic relationship.

After concluding that this earlier Court ruling rendered our law unconstitutional, I vetoed the law. I pointed to my constitutional duty,
under the oath I had taken, and the futility—from the standpoint of
protecting unborn human life—of passing laws which had no chance
of ever taking effect to help the unborn.

This is what I said in my veto message:

> [O]ur concerns cannot end with protecting unborn children, but must
> extend to protecting, and promoting the health, of *all* our children, and
> their mothers. The right to life must mean the right to a decent life. Our
> concern for future mothers must include a concern for current mothers.
> Our respect for the wonders of pregnancy must be equalled by a sensitivity
> to the traumas of pregnancy. This Administration has called for significantly
> increased support for child and maternal health programs, for education,
> for rape counseling and support services. And we will continue to advance
> more programs born of the recognition that our moral responsibility to
> mothers and children does not end at birth. These proposals deserve to re-
> ceive the same overwhelming vote of approval in the Legislature that this
> bill received.
>
> Let me re-state in summary the distinction between personal belief and
> constitutional duty as it applies to this legislation. I believe abortion to be
> the ultimate violence. I believe strongly that *Roe* v. *Wade* was incorrectly

decided as a matter of law and represents a national public policy both divisive and destructive. It has unleashed a tidal wave that has swept away the lives of millions of defenseless, innocent unborn children. In according the woman's right of privacy in the abortion decision both exclusivity and finality, the Supreme Court has not only disregarded the right of the unborn child to life itself, but has deprived parents, spouses, and the state of the right to participate in a decision in which they all have a vital interest. This interest ought to be protected, rather than denied, by the law. This policy has had, and will continue to have, a profoundly destructive effect upon the fabric of American life. But these personal beliefs must yield to the duty, imposed by my oath of office, to follow the Constitution as interpreted by the Supreme Court of the United States. . . .

Most importantly, I emphasize that we must—and we will—enact a strong and sustainable Abortion Control Act that forms a humane and constitutional foundation for our efforts to ensure that no child is denied his or her right to walk in the sun and make the most out of life. I will sign this bill when it reaches the end of the legislative process and attains those standards.

Following the veto, my staff and I worked closely with pro-life groups and legislative leaders to draft the Abortion Control Act of 1989 within the framework of Supreme Court cases, including *Webster*. The law required parental consent for minors, informed consent, and a twenty-four-hour waiting period. These limitations were upheld in *Planned Parenthood of Southeastern Pennsylvania* v. *Casey*. A spousal notification requirement in the law was struck down. It had required notification of the child's father if he was married to the mother, unlike the earlier provision I had opposed which required notification of the father, whether or not a spouse, and which had previously been rejected by the Court.

Thus, while concluding that my oath of office prevented me from signing an unconstitutional law, I also recognized a right, and a duty, to work to change the law within the democratic process. First, by enacting a law that was designed to limit and reduce abortions within the constitutional authority of the states. Second, to speak out in favor of the protection of human life so as to influence others, including federal and state leaders.

That was how I saw my duty then. Now, eight years later, I feel compelled to inquire further: What exactly *is* the relationship between the rulings of the United States Supreme Court and the Constitution a governor is bound to uphold?

The Court can be—and has been—seriously wrong. The Court erred in the case of *Dred Scott v. Sanford*, which upheld the practice of slavery. And I believe that the Court erred in the case of *Roe v. Wade*.

Thinking back on my veto decision, I now incline more to Abraham Lincoln's attitude toward *Dred Scott*, which he and others at the time viewed as disastrously wrong. Lincoln viewed the ruling as "not having quite established a settled doctrine for the country." In his debates with Stephen Douglas, Lincoln derided the Little Giant's view that every Supreme Court opinion should be embraced as valid for all eternity— as if judicial opinions were holy writ to be heard as, "Thus saith the Lord." A year-and-a-half after the *Dred Scott* decision, Lincoln said: "If I were in Congress, and a vote should come up on a question whether slavery should be prohibited in the new territories, in spite of the *Dred Scott* decision, I would vote that it should." Several years later, Congress did precisely that. In open defiance of *Dred Scott* Congress outlawed slavery in the territories.

In his first inaugural address, Lincoln referred to the *Dred Scott* case, expressing the view that other officers of the government could not be obligated to accept any new laws created by the Court unless they, too, were persuaded by the force of the Court's reasoning. Any other position would mean, in his view, that "the policies of the government upon vital questions, affecting the whole people, [could] be irrevocably fixed by decisions of the Supreme Court, the instant they are made, in ordinary litigation between parties, in personal actions." If that were to occur, said Lincoln, "the people will have ceased to be their own rulers, having to that extent practically resigned the government into the hands of that eminent tribunal."

In other words, as Lincoln saw it, a Supreme Court decision did not irrevocably end the matter: the Congress could, by legislation, change the law as announced by the Court. And there is good authority for the position that, since the Court in *Roe v. Wade* did not decide when life begins, the Congress could find as a fact that life begins at conception; and decree that the unborn child is entitled to legal protection under the Fourteenth Amendment.

In *Casey*, the Court had affirmed the general principle that there could be limits placed on the practice of abortion. Interestingly, Planned Parenthood had chosen not to challenge two provisions of our law: the provision banning so-called "gender-selection" abortions, and the provision outlawing abortions after twenty-four weeks of gestation except in cases where the mother's life was in jeopardy. That decision not to challenge these provisions was, I believe, a purely tactical one. It was a smart public relations move: Had these provisions come to light, many Americans would be amazed to learn that such abortions were legal. Planned Parenthood lawyers, fearing the wrath of the people, did not have the gumption to stand before the Supreme Court to argue that gender selection or third-trimester abortions were in the public interest. Sensing this weakness, they preferred to drop the subject altogether— which they did.

What I remember most about the day on which arguments were heard—April 22, 1992—was my arrival and my departure. Arriving, I stepped out into the gray parking area under the Supreme Court building. I had a flashback of being on that same spot years earlier as a law clerk sent off on a research assignment for Covington & Burling. Like every young lawyer, I had notions then of the day when I would return to actually argue a case before the highest court in the land. It had never occurred to me that I might instead return as a litigant, especially in such a high-profile case.

As we departed the courtroom after the arguments, I could hear muffled noise coming from the plaza in front of the building, where groups from both camps were staging protests. We walked down the long, marble steps in front of the court building and I could see ahead of me dozens of television cameras and microphones. At that moment, pressed for comment, I tried to lay aside all the familiar arguments in the debate and ask the one question I believed to be at the heart of the issue: "In this debate, who speaks for the child? Today I've come here to say that *Pennsylvania* speaks for the child."

And that was the question I wanted to ask my fellow Democrats at the convention in Madison Square Garden: Amid all the bitterness and clamor over abortion, who speaks for the child?

I had been to many Democratic Party conventions before—always memorable. I remember like it was yesterday, striding proudly down the Boardwalk in Atlantic City in 1964 with my alternate-delegate badge pinned on my suit jacket, on my way to the opening session of the convention that would nominate Lyndon Johnson for president, and approaching a solitary figure standing off in a corner near the entrance to the convention hall. He introduced himself as Senator Eugene McCarthy. That night we heard the haunting speech of Robert Kennedy, whose brother had been killed just seven months before. I had introduced RFK at his first public speech after his brother's death. Speaking at a dinner of the Friendly Sons of St. Patrick in Scranton in March of 1964, he had read the old Irish poem about the great liberator of Ireland, Owen O'Neill, who died young:

> *Sagest in the council was he,*
> *kindest in the Hall:*
> *Sure we never won a battle*
> *—'twas Owen won them all*
> *Soft as woman's was your voice, O'Neill:*
> *bright was your eye,*
> *Oh! why did you leave us, Owen?*
> *Why did you die?*
> *Your troubles are all over,*
> *you're at rest with God on high,*
> *But we're slaves and we're orphans, Owen!*
> *—why did you die?*

A hush had fallen over the room in Scranton when Bob Kennedy moved to his conclusion. "On this St. Patrick's evening, let me urge you one final time to recall the heritage of the Irish. Let us hold out our hands to those who struggle for freedom today—at home and abroad—as Ireland struggled for a thousand years."

In 1968 I had the honor of announcing a unanimous vote of the Pennsylvania delegation for Senator Edmund Muskie, the vice presidential nominee, whose father lived for a time in Dickson City just outside of Scranton. By then, of course, Gene McCarthy was no longer a solitary figure and Bobby Kennedy was gone.

I missed the 1972 convention in Miami where George McGovern was nominated. I admired McGovern personally but wasn't thrilled by his nomination. If one good thing came of that election year, it was the selection (after all the confusion surrounding Senator Thomas Eagleton, his first selection) of Sargent Shriver for the number-two spot. I regarded the presence of Shriver on the ticket as at least one redeeming aspect of the whole fiasco. When Shriver came through Pennsylvania during the 1972 campaign, a lot of elected officials preferred not to be seen with him. Those seeking re-election knew that electoral disaster was imminent; they feared being dragged down by the national ticket; they had a lot to lose, none more than I. Running for re-election as auditor general, my name appeared next to "McGovern–Shriver" on the ballot—right in the crosshairs. But I was out there, proud to stand by Shriver, who remains to this day a good friend. (It was there I also met a young aide of his named Mark Shields, now a well-known political commentator.) To shy away from our candidate, I felt, would have been to desert the Democratic Party.

From that year until 1992, I had supported every nominee with varying degrees of enthusiasm, to the point of heading up the Pennsylvania contingent for presidential nominee Michael Dukakis in 1988 in Atlanta. I didn't take the view, "My party, right or wrong!" But I believed in the Democratic Party. It may go wrong now and then. I may not always favor one or another nominee. But it claimed my allegiance. It was my political home.

Describing the 1992 convention, I hardly know where to begin. It was like nothing I have ever seen before or since.

The theme of it all was "unity" and "inclusion." We were all portrayed by the convention choreographers as a giant "circle of friends," with a winning ticket at long last within our reach. There was even a song by that name, which we were all to sing—"Let's build a circle of friends. . . ."—while holding hands and swaying back and forth. My family and I, standing there with my press aide, Karen Chandler, declined to join in. We watched the scene with utter bewilderment: for the first time in my life, I felt a total sense of estrangement from my own party. The pretense of inclusion was contradicted by the reality.

A few months earlier I had appeared before the Democratic Platform Committee in Cleveland. There were many Democrats, I said, who opposed our party's embrace of the radical pro-abortion lobby. Often it seemed the Democratic National Committee had become little more than an auxiliary of NARAL—the National Abortion Rights Action League. I was living proof of this division in the party, I pointed out. A pro-life Democrat, I had just been re-elected governor by a margin of one million votes, defeating a pro-choice Republican. And by electing Harris Wofford, Pennsylvania had given the national Democratic Party the momentum it needed to take on President Bush.

As for "women's issues," I added, I would gladly compare my record with any governor in the country: I had appointed more women to my cabinet and other key jobs than any other Democratic governor. I had championed a wide range of nutrition, healthcare, and economic-opportunity programs for women, children, and families. And I had given unprecedented support to programs to fight abuse of women across Pennsylvania, funding domestic abuse and rape-crisis programs at unprecedented levels. No one needed to tell me about the problems facing women: I had spent six years doing something about them. But I did not regard abortion as a benefit to anyone, least of all the women of America, who for twenty years had been exploited, used, and misled by the abortion industry. Young mothers and their children, I pointed out, were the natural constituency of the Democratic Party. They were people in need of our support, compassion, and love. Abortion-on-demand was no solution. There were honest and profound differences within the party that had to be addressed. We needed to face up to them and debate the issue, not smother our consciences in a shroud of "unity."

How, I concluded, could this party, which claimed to leave no one out and no one behind, abandon the most vulnerable and defenseless member of the human family—the unborn child?

I hadn't really expected a standing ovation from the committee, made up of fervent pro-choice supporters. So the next step was to write a letter to Ronald Brown, the party chairman, requesting an opportunity to address the convention in New York. "The platform [committee] draft," I wrote in my July 2 letter to Brown, ". . . has the effect of placing the national party even more squarely within the abortion-on-demand camp. I believe this is a serious mistake for the party and would like the opportunity to present this point of view, shared by many Democrats, to the convention."

Brown never responded to my letter. Arriving at the convention, I had another letter hand-delivered to Texas Governor Anne Richards on July 13. She was chairperson of the convention. No answer from Richards, either. Eventually, I received a carbon copy of a letter—not even addressed to me —from the parliamentarian of the convention to the general counsel for the Democratic National Committee, denying my request to speak because it was out of order. The kind of letter they might have sent Lyndon LaRouche, had he asked to address the convention.

It's hard to be detached about my experience at the convention that year. But let me make the effort and simply note that I thought this was a strange way to treat the Democratic governor of Pennsylvania.

I understood, of course, the politics of the situation. Our presidential nominee was pro-choice. Despite having once approved an Arkansas law banning third-trimester abortions, and claiming to be pro-life, Governor Clinton was now firmly in the pro-choice camp. Our vice-presidential nominee was pro-choice. As a congressman and senator from Tennessee, Al Gore, too, had once been pro-life. But all that had changed. He was also on a clearly pro-choice ticket, relying on groups like NARAL for support. The Clinton camp did not want a lot of rancor and argument over the issue at the convention.

All that understood, I wasn't looking to stir up rancor. I merely wanted a chance to speak, to offer a strong dissent based on the party's historic commitment to protecting the powerless. Why was that such a threat? If we were truly the party of "tolerance" and "inclusion," as the convention speakers claimed—just a great big circle of friends—what was the problem?

I leave it for the historians to check, but I don't recall any precedent for this situation except, perhaps, the 1968 Chicago Convention when dissenters had been excluded. Some of the party's finest moments had come about in convention debates. Think of Harry Truman in 1948, at the historic Philadelphia convention. As a practical political matter, it sure didn't help the national ticket any when Hubert Humphrey, the young mayor of Minneapolis, got up and urged the inclusion of a civil-rights plank in the Democratic platform. The result was that Strom Thurmond of South Carolina got up and took a walk, carrying off a lot of Southern votes with him when he formed the Dixiecrat Party.

The easier way would have been for President Truman, hailing from a Southern border state himself, to keep Humphrey as far from the microphone as possible and in some way finesse the issue. But Truman didn't do that. He let Humphrey speak. They didn't hide their differences in empty feel-good talk of "friends" and "tolerance": They debated principle. And, what is more important, Truman stood on principle. The civil-rights plank was put into the platform.

Or take the 1968 convention in Chicago. Supposedly this had been a formative experience for the generation running the party in 1992. The nominee, Humphrey, had supported the Vietnam War. He was opposed by anti-war protestors who demanded the right to be heard. The party establishment, led by Mayor Richard Daley, had refused to let the protesters speak, and so there were riots and shouting and marches outside the convention hall. The great lesson of all this was supposedly that dissent should be tolerated, even welcomed, and not silenced.

Finally, consider the Republican National Convention of 1992 in Houston. It is now routinely described in the media as an intolerant, "hate-filled" convention, marked by ominous talk of "religious wars." But I'll say this for the Republicans: At least they allowed dissent. President Bush and Vice President Quayle were both firmly pro-life. But all the same, Labor Secretary Lynn Martin, Massachusetts Governor William Weld, and various other pro-choice Republicans were permitted to get up there and express their differences without any threats of mass unrest. There were no walkouts or threats or shouting matches. They spoke, and that was that. The Republican candidates were confident enough of their beliefs to permit dissent.

I believe that what happened at the 1992 Democratic convention reflects a deep insecurity over the abortion issue among Democrats. If there were such unanimity on the issue, they would not fear open debate. Deep down, I believe even the most self-assured pro-choice Democrats sense that something is not right, that their cause fits uneasily into the vision of the Democratic Party. That vision was expressed in a full-page ad which I organized, entitled "The New American Compact," which ran in *The New York Times* on July 14, the day the convention was to adopt the abortion-on-demand plank. It was cosigned by Democrats and Republicans, liberals and conservatives, including former New York Governor Hugh Carey, Sargent and Eunice Shriver, Harvard Professor Mary Ann Glendon, former Treasury Secretary William Simon, liberal journalist Nat Hentoff, and many others. Here, in part, is what the ad said:

The first two hundred years of the American Republic tell an unfolding tale of aspiration—and progress—toward the ideal of liberty and justice for all. This progress has been rapid in some periods, halting in others; sometimes it has suffered setbacks. But from the early days of the American colonies to our own time, the basic trajectory was consistent and seemingly inexorable. The boundaries of the community of the commonly protected were steadily expanded—and the story of America became the story of an evermore inclusive society. The United States welcomed its immigrants, protected its workers, freed the slaves, enfranchised women, aided the needy, provided social security for the aged, ensured the civil rights of all its citizens and made public spaces available to the handicapped: "all in service to its ideals of justice."

Then, in January 1973, the U.S. Supreme Court . . . drastically reversed this pattern of expanding inclusion. . . . [S]even unelected justices performed the most momentous act of exclusion in our history: they deprived every human being, for the first nine months of his or her life, of the most fundamental human right of all—the right to life.

The labor movement and child-labor laws, the civil-rights movement, equal opportunity for women—these were the causes around which Democrats first came together. And every one of us could explain why: because we believed in helping the powerless, protecting the vulnerable.

But the abortion cause is different. It's hard to think of anything more foreign to the principles of the Democratic Party or the whole American experience. Far from being "inclusive," it excludes an entire class of fellow human beings from our care and protection. It's the only constitutional right we're ashamed of, avoiding the word *abortion* with contorted euphemisms like "reproductive rights" and "termination" and "evacuation." Far from liberating women, abortion has become a lucrative industry, exploiting young women beyond anything ever imagined. When pregnancy comes at a difficult time, which is the worthier response of society: To surround mother and child alike with protection and love, or to hold out the cold comfort of an abortion clinic? Where is America's true character to be seen—in an adoptive home or at the abortion clinic? In which role is a woman more empowered—giving life or taking it?

These are questions that rest uneasily on the conscience of today's Democratic Party. We have traded our principles for power—the fleeting power offered by loud and well-financed factions like NARAL and Planned Parenthood. But as we saw in 1994, that power is just about used up. In its bargain with the abortion industry were the seeds of the party's undoing. Today the party is imploding, with mass defections not seen in American politics since the demise of the Whigs in the 1850s. It is losing the allegiance of voters for one very simple reason, much deeper than our views on taxes or the budget or any particular program: It is a party that has lost its soul.

After my banishment from the Garden, Republicans saw political benefit to themselves in having me deliver at their convention the speech I wanted to give in New York. I appreciated the thought, but wasn't about to be trotted out in Houston as the

Democratic poster boy for the Republican Party. The weekend before the election, just after the Democratic governor of Maryland, William Donald Schaefer, had endorsed President Bush, I counted seven phone calls from White House Chief of Staff John Sununu, who apparently thought I might do the same. All went unreturned. (In light of the Republicans' waffling on the abortion issue, my decision looks better every day.)

Back in New York, though, the Democrats had different ideas about party loyalty. Not only would I be barred from speaking, a special fate had been prepared for me: I would be publicly humiliated by my own party.

One of the night's platform guests would be a woman named Kathy Taylor. She was a pro-choice activist from Pennsylvania, a *Republican* who had helped in the campaign of my Republican opponent, Barbara Hafer. When I heard she would be on the platform as an honored guest, I just couldn't believe it.

Nor was this the only insult I had to endure because of my pro-life position. There were more surprises in store for me. Karen Ritter, a Democratic legislator from Pennsylvania, was selling large buttons featuring a picture of me dressed up as the Pope. Every now and then, I would see people wearing these same buttons, apparently their idea of a joke. To me, it was simply a case of anti-Catholic bigotry. What was going on here? What had become of the Democratic Party I once knew?

Our assigned seats were in what as a kid I used to call the "nosebleed section." From there Ellen, our children, and I had a good view of the assembly—this whole "circle of friends" standing up and shouting and applauding each speaker. "Let's remember this moment," I said to Ellen. "One day, it's all going to come back around." It is happening already: Most of those elected officials who orchestrated the '92 convention have since been driven from public life by the vote of the people. Others seem headed for a similar fate.

For all the talk of "diversity" within the party, I have never seen a more rigid, predictable, or doctrinaire group of people in my life. Nor have I have felt such deep, bitter hatred—the tyranny of the far left, up close and personal. One after another the speakers would incant the same pieties, each time getting a rise out of the crowd. All a speaker had to do was end every other sentence or so with the phrase ". . . a woman's right to choose!" and the audience went wild. The mere mention of those words, or variations such as ". . . the right to privacy!" or ". . . reproductive rights!" could make even the most lackluster speaker stand up there feeling like a spellbinder.

Then came Kathy Taylor, sharing the podium with five other pro-choice women. And so from my seat in the outer reaches of the Garden, I watched a pro-choice Republican supporter of my pro-choice Republican opponent, whom I had defeated by a million votes to be re-elected as Democratic governor, proudly proclaiming her allegiance to the pro-choice forces.

When Pennsylvania's turn came to announce to the convention its vote for president, I didn't feel much calling, as the delegation's leader, to fill that traditional role. I declined the honor, asking a friend—state senator and Democratic state chairman Bill Lincoln—to do it in my stead.

The next day, Senator Al Gore called me to say that Governor Clinton had played no role in denying me the right to speak. I knew both Gore and Clinton from earlier years when Gore was running for president in 1988. He had sought my support. I knew Clinton from his time as governor of Arkansas. Governor Clinton had once been our houseguest at the governor's residence in Harrisburg. Senator Gore offered to put Governor Clinton on the phone if I preferred to hear it from him. That wasn't necessary, I told him. I'd accept his word on the matter. But who *was* behind the refusal to hear my views? Gore couldn't give me an answer. The question has gone unanswered to this day.

The official line from the convention publicity machine was that I was not permitted to speak because I hadn't endorsed Clinton. But if that's the case, why had Kathleen Brown, state treasurer of California and sister of presidential hopeful Jerry Brown, been permitted to address the convention? She hadn't endorsed the nominee, either.

As for Kathy Taylor, reporters later asked her how her invitation came about. She said she had been invited to speak by NARAL, which then, she explained, had cleared it with the Democratic National Committee. The whole thing was quite deliberate. And whatever the nominees thought of her presence on the podium, apparently no one saw fit to object.

But there was one bright spot at the convention. A Minnesota delegate came up to me and gave me a big red button which I wore each night into the convention sessions. Inscribed on the button in large white letters were these words:

I AM A PRO-LIFE DEMOCRAT.
I WANT MY PARTY BACK!

Not a bad rallying cry for the future. To me, it bears the only hope for a party that seems to have lost its moral bearings, its sense of calling. I cannot claim to bring any special prophetic gifts to the abortion issue. But I do know this. I have never in my life sensed such anger and hatred as at that convention. However the abortion issue is resolved, it will not be resolved by anger and hatred and bitterness. At its heart is a question of who we are as a people, what we stand for, where we're bound. The question America is struggling with today is not when life begins— science long ago answered that. The question is when love begins—who shall be included in the circle of humanity, the human family.

All the shouting, cheering, laughing, and hissing I heard that night at our convention was still not loud enough to silence that question which keeps coming back: Who speaks for the child?

17

Gratitude

When I first saw her, no words were called for. We said
nothing, we just held each other tight.

EACH DAY, I felt a little stronger. Each day, I appreciated the very fact
of being. Even with the little discomforts, every morning—rain or
shine—was glorious. But it wasn't just a general, diffuse gratitude: I felt
the weight of one particular debt, my debt to Frances Lucas. It was time
to meet her.

Ellen had written Mrs. Lucas a personal note upon learning her
name just after the surgery. Ordinarily we would not have learned her
name at all. These things were usually kept anonymous. We had also
talked to her on the phone. But we wanted to have a private, personal
meeting with her, and at a time and place convenient to her. That
meant waiting a while.

Understandably, Mrs. Lucas and I had felt the whole experience in
different ways. I was feeling the glory of it all in each new day, and I
think she was touched by that gift to me. In our brief conversation, she
could not have been more gracious or encouraging. But at the end of
the day, she was still a mother grieving for a lost son.

Long before our paths crossed, Mrs. Lucas had known more than her share of grief. Her father, a coal miner in West Virginia, had died when she was three. When she was ten, the family house burned to the ground. Frances and her five brothers and sisters were left scattered in different homes across the neighborhood. Her mother was a housekeeper for a man and his invalid son. He built a five-room house and gave it to the Lucas family for thirty-five dollars a month. In Monessen, she had opened her home to neighborhood children, black and white, in need of a meal or a place to sleep. This was the woman God chose to decide my fate that evening in 1993.

In due time the day and place of our meeting were set. Later Ellen and I would invite her husband, Alvin, and their daughter, Yvonne, to have dinner with us at the governor's residence in Harrisburg. But this first meeting was to be as simple and private as possible. We agreed to meet at the William Penn Hotel in Pittsburgh, where I'd met with my doctors almost a year earlier.

No one was there with me, waiting in the hotel room that afternoon, but Ellen and Matt. It was a very emotional moment for me. What do you say? Mrs. Lucas had said that she believed her son continued to live on in the good things I might do, and that comforted me. Still, I strained to come up with the right words to express my feelings the first moment I saw her.

As it turned out, when I first saw her, no words were called for. We said nothing, we just held each other tight. I'm a somewhat formal person, but it was the most natural thing in the world to embrace her. Keeping me alive was her own son's heart, a heart formed within her own body. Life had passed from her, to him, to me. I really don't know how to express it except that I felt, beyond just plain gratitude, a spiritual union with Mrs. Lucas. It was a moment beyond tears.

Then there were hugs and embraces all around. Ellen embraced her next, then Matt. We all sat down and talked like old friends: How was I feeling? Would she and her husband like to have dinner with Ellen and me at the residence? Later, she would say it was like meeting family.

I've had a lot of time since then to turn it all over in my mind. Sometimes I've wondered if I would have responded as Frances Lucas did to the crisis. If I had just found my son bleeding to death, had just watched him crying in his final moments on a hospital bed, would I have found it in myself to think of someone else? Maybe, but I'm not sure.

In a way, Mrs. Lucas is the one person in the story not bound to me by obligation, professional or personal. We had no ties at all except as fellow human beings, strangers on the same journey. She could have asked the people who approached her about donating her son's organs to please go away, please let her grieve in peace, and no one would ever blame her. Somehow, in the darkness of her son's hospital room she brought light to mine. I owe her my life. She saved me with her love. For as many more years as her gift carries me, I will be grateful.

To a *New York Times* reporter, Dr. Starzl described my story this way:

> "He was like a guy in a tiny prison and all by himself, and with no help from anyone, he figured a way to get out. It was remarkable how he grabbed on to the last rung of life on his way down the chute and pulled himself back to the top."

He was being a little modest. How many souls reaching for that last rung look up to find people like Tom Starzl or Frances Lucas looking down? I have never believed in the idea of the self-made man. Now I know there is no such thing as the self-saved man. We need each other. It just becomes a lot clearer from the bottom rung. Without loving and being loved, none of us can ever make it up there to the top.

18

The Last Rung

*I felt at times less like a candidate with an agenda than a
witness with a story. I sensed that millions of people across
America would respond to my message. . . . A message offered to the country because of its importance to America's
future. A message everyone could understand and feel deep
in their own hearts.*

IN APRIL 1995 I was sitting in the Arlington, Virginia, offices of some
advisors preparing for an interview the following week with Mike
Wallace of 60 *Minutes*. They would fire questions at me, Wallace style,
and I would respond. My son, Matt, was there, too, firing away with
abandon.

I had just formed an exploratory committee for the 1996 presidential
campaign. "Exploratory" means just that. You may run, but you're not
yet sure. You explore the race from every angle: Can the necessary
money be raised? Is there broad support for your ideas, your message?
Are you prepared to make the enormous personal commitment the effort will require? The exploratory committee allows the prospective
candidate to find answers to these questions before you actually enter
the race.

And that is all I was doing—exploring. No press conferences. No
promotion. Just a simple news release announcing the filing of the committee. But these quiet steps only seemed to make the press that much

more curious. I was the only Democrat actually considering a challenge to an incumbent president. Our phones were ringing off the hook.

We decided to do the *60 Minutes* interview. It would be followed by dozens of other TV appearances—*Meet the Press, Face the Nation, Larry King Live*. On Easter Sunday morning the producers and camera crew of *60 Minutes* were in our living room to get some footage of the family. The crew followed us to church and, later in the day, filmed us having dinner at my daughter Kate's house. They would travel with me the next day, Monday, to Pittsburgh, where I was to promote "Organ Donor Awareness Week." The plan was for the crew to return to my home for more filming on Tuesday, followed by still more filming later that week at our campaign headquarters in Arlington. It was a taste of what a presidential campaign would be like. The Wallace encounter would be my Rubicon. Preparation was crucial. The tough questions had to be asked and answered.

"Governor, you have just been through a heart and liver transplant. You're lucky to be alive. Do you really think you're ready to run for president?"

"My doctors have given me a clean bill of health. They've said it's okay for me to do this, that I can look forward to a normal life expectancy. And bear in mind that I ran the state of Pennsylvania—didn't miss a day of work—from late December 1993 until January 1995. But you know, the larger question here is the health of our society, of America itself. . . ."

The session went on like this for several hours, my advisors interrupting me, trying to knock me off keel, all doing their best imitation of the inquisitorial Wallace manner. Such sessions are the standard infield practice for political candidates facing an important interview or debate. I had been through similar preparations in all of my campaigns, but none in which the stakes were so high. This interview would be seen by millions across the country. And most of the viewers would be seeing me for the first time. It would be a defining moment.

"Governor, in the coming campaign, will Reginald McFadden be your 'Willie Horton'?"

"McFadden had been in prison for twenty-four years; his release was recommended to me by the Pardons Board, the commissioner of corrections, even the sentencing judge. Horton was still serving his sentence when he was released on what amounted to a weekend pass. The two cases are as different as night and day. But for my part, the important thing is to accept full responsibility for my decision—which I do."

"Governor, at the 1992 Democratic convention, you were barred from speaking. Is this personal? Are you just out to settle a few scores?"

"This campaign will be about the future of America, and my party's vision of what our future holds. A presidential campaign, after all, is a tremendous undertaking. It will take everything I have, every ounce of strength and commitment. I would not make that effort merely to settle a score. Democrats who join me will be taking a big risk of their own, going up against an incumbent president and their party leadership. I would not ask that of anyone unless there was something much greater at stake here. . . ."

"Abortion. You have very strong feelings about it, Governor. Isn't this just a single-issue candidacy?"

"No, Mike, it's not. I expect to hear that charge a lot from my opponents, so let me just put them on notice right now: This will be a broad-based campaign touching on many issues. It will be about putting the American family back at the center of all domestic policy in this country. It will be about the middle-class squeeze and the decline in real family income, and all the resulting economic and moral costs of that decline. It will be about overhauling a federal tax code hostile to working families, and relieving the crushing burden of the Social Security tax on working families. It will be about welfare reform which requires work, but does not penalize the child. It will be about making adoption a top national priority. And yes, it will be about protecting the most helpless and innocent among us, the unborn child. In 1996—"

"Come now, Governor. You are pro-life in a pro-choice party. You're a devout Catholic who believes—"

"Let me stop you right there, Mike. Why is it that reporters so frequently identify my religion? In the papers it's always 'Casey, a devout Catholic. . .' You don't read stories saying, 'Dole, a devout

Methodist . . .' or 'Clinton, a devout Baptist. . .' But because I'm pro-life, my religion is always thrown in there like some little code word to the reader saying, 'Watch out for this guy. He's *Catholic!* He's one of *those* people.'

"Well, let me tell you something: This is not a Catholic issue. It's not a religious issue. It's not a gender issue. It's a question about humanity, about America, about what kind of people we are and what we believe. . . ."

"Governor, have you looked at the polls lately? How can you claim to speak for the majority when, in point of fact, the polls show that most Americans favor a woman's right to choose?"

"Let me answer you with a question of my own. What defines the Democratic Party? At our core, what do we believe in? I believe the core of the Democratic Party, our guiding idea, is a belief in lifting up the broken, protecting the helpless, welcoming the stranger. On the issue of protecting human life, the national Democratic Party for the first time in its history has taken the side of the powerful against the powerless. And so today our party has abandoned its central mission. As for those polls, Mike, let's start with Pennsylvania. . . ."

On and on it went, with a lunch break followed by another round. I was handling the questions pretty well—easy enough when it's not really Mike Wallace there going for the jugular. The mood was hopeful and earnest. This was it, the big game, time to put my convictions to the test.

Some friends, Democrats and Republicans alike, had first come to me with the idea to run for president two years earlier. I heard them out. It wasn't the first time the thought had entered my mind. But their overture—though they had no way of knowing this—was not well-timed. They came to Harrisburg to pitch the idea just after I learned of my health problems. As they laid out their grand plan, I remember thinking, "My God, why am I even *listening* to this?"

Time passed, Dr. Starzl had appeared, I'd survived the transplant, finished my second term with a bang, and now here we were again—only weeks or months away from the moment of truth. A run for the presidency.

And then there had been the reaction of the White House to my exploratory committee.

"Governor Casey of Pennsylvania has formed an exploratory committee to consider a run for the Democratic nomination. What's your reaction?" reporters had asked White House Press Secretary Mike McCurry.

McCurry said something about not wanting to talk about the politics of the campaign just yet. Too early. That would come next year. But, he concluded, "I would find it hard, in any event, to muster any enthusiasm for comment on something so insignificant."

A tittering could be heard in the background from the White House press corps. When I saw McCurry's response on the news that night, his words and manner reminded me of everything that needed changing in American politics. Here, in eighteen words, was the arrogance of power. I made a note to hold onto the McCurry news clip for use in our TV ads in New Hampshire.

Meanwhile, other flacks for the party establishment were working overtime putting out the same line. It was all "insignificant." After hearing this line again and again on the news, it was clear to me that we were on the right track. *They doth protest too much*, I thought.

On March 26, a few days after McCurry's dismissal of my candidacy, White House Chief of Staff Leon Panetta appeared on *Meet the Press* and was questioned by moderator Tim Russert about my possible campaign. "As you know, [Governor Casey] is against abortion rights, as are millions of Democrats throughout the country. And the official White House statement to Governor Casey's announcement was, 'This is insignificant.' Isn't that insulting to anti-abortion rights Democrats across the country?"

"Well," replied Panetta, "I think what the comment referred to is the fact the he has started an exploratory committee, not made the decision that he wants to run. And it was basically indicating that that particular event was something we're going to see a lot of over these next few months, as individuals establish those kinds of committees. . . ."

A non-answer. They would have to do better than that.

On April 9 Russert put the same question to Vice President Gore. "Do you take a challenge by a two-term governor of Pennsylvania lightly?"

"No, I sure don't. We sure don't. And the president doesn't agree with that characterization at all. And nor do I. He is a man of substance. I happen to be a personal friend of his, and the president has immense respect for him."

Finally, President Clinton was asked on CNN to comment on my candidacy. His response suggested he had given some thought to the matter:

> Bob Casey is a man I served with as governor. I have a high regard for him and I have a lot of respect for him. And I kept in pretty close touch with him and his family when he went through his medical problems. I think he is a remarkable, resilient person. He is a committed, anti-abortion, anti-choice person who has served with distinction in government. We agree on many, many issues. I believe you can be pro-choice and anti-abortion. He doesn't believe that. He believes that the Democratic Party has been badly hurt by the abortion issue and that it's more important than any other issue. And he believes that with a real depth of conviction. And he will have to do whatever he thinks is right. And he will do that. I'm sure he will do whatever he thinks is right. I think when you look at the alternatives between the Democrats and the Republicans and the fact that the Republicans seem to like to—it's hard to know where they really stand on that issue. They talk one way and act another. I would hope that he would think about that and think about what would happen in the event of a campaign. But that's his decision and whatever he does I will respect.

Behind these carefully chosen words was a simple, hard fact: A challenge by a two-term Democratic governor from a must-win state like Pennsylvania, a campaign to help working families across America and protect human life, posed a serious threat to the re-election of the president. I knew this. And I knew *they* knew.

Not long after I formed the committee, I was in Washington at a social gathering and met an old friend who had ties to the White House.

"You're causing quite a stir these days," he said, referring to the publicity my possible candidacy had received. Then he leaned toward me, and, making sure he was not overheard, said, "They're scared to death." There was no question who "they" were.

And "they" had good reason to be concerned, because the values my candidacy would represent were driving the political dynamic of the country. The national Democrats had just been wiped out in the 1994 general election. Traditional Democrats across the country were fleeing to the other side, even in Congress. I had predicted as much in the weeks before that election. It didn't take any special prophetic powers to see what was coming. The election would turn on much deeper questions than tax policy or even the broader economic or pocket-book issues, important as those might be. All over America, people were deeply concerned about what they saw as the unraveling of our values, the general drift of our culture, the violent and debased spirit that seemed to be overtaking us. As concerned as they were about our fiscal deficit, they were far more troubled by our moral deficit.

In that national debate, the leaders of my party had lost standing, lost the confidence and respect of the people. More by default than any particular merit of their own, Republicans would reap the rewards. I told a Baltimore audience on October 22, 1994, just before the congressional elections:

> Without question, there's something fundamental and dramatic stirring across the heartland of this country. It's that wave I've talked about. It's palpable—you can feel it. If you're in politics and you can't feel that wave, you're in the wrong business. You ought to be selling life insurance or doing something else, but you shouldn't be in politics, because it's there. You can taste it. And I think the people on the other side are beginning to taste it too. Beginning to feel it. Beginning to feel the hot breath of the people. Because character is important. Values are important, and people care about them. They vote that way, thank God. Without question, something dramatic is happening. We're witnesses to what I think is a revolution. Something which gives me great hope and confidence in the future is quietly and slowly but inexorably changing. . . .

The election of 1994 and every poll since then has borne out that prediction.

But deeper than any polling data, I had a feeling about 1996—the same feeling I had ten years earlier in 1986, when no one gave me a chance of winning.

Around the country were men and women just like me, who felt as I did about our party and what had become of it. We might not agree on every last question. But we were all yearning for the conviction and vision Democrats once stood for. With them were millions more Republicans equally disillusioned with their party and its perpetual wavering and equivocation. All the polls continue to show that a majority of the American people would vote for a credible third-party candidate for president, further evidence of what I'm talking about.

Sitting in that Arlington office in April 1995, just across the Potomac from Washington, D.C., I wasn't sure I was the best person to give voice to these ideas. But if others were going to do it, where were they now? It seemed to fall to me by default. Of two things, I felt absolutely certain: Winning the nomination from an incumbent president would be the hardest undertaking of my life. But it was doable.

Many people—most people—would react with disbelief to that last statement. "How can that be?" they would say. I know that some of my best friends were completely taken aback when I formed the exploratory committee. "Why is he doing this? He's recovering from a heart and liver transplant! Why doesn't he just quit while he's ahead? And besides, he can never beat Bill Clinton. Bill Clinton is an incumbent president!"

In a way, for me it was—in Yogi Berra's oft-quoted words—"Déjà vu all over again." All you have to do is substitute the electoral improbability of a three-time loser for that of a heart-liver transplant recipient. All you have to do is substitute Bill Scranton for Bill Clinton, and you have 1986 all over again.

I understood the shock and amazement expressed by my friends at the idea of my running for president. But I had an entirely different reading about my prospects. The reason had to do with me only indirectly. It had everything to do with the power of the ideas and values my candidacy would have harnessed. I guess it came down to a different vision of what the people of this country really wanted, and where our country should be going.

Many people discount the power of the so-called "cultural issues"—

and especially of the abortion issue. I see it just the other way around: These issues are central to the national resurgence of the Republicans, central to the national implosion of the Democrats, central to the question of whether there will be a third party. The national Democrats may, and probably will, get a temporary bump in the polls—even, perhaps, one more national election victory—from their reactive strategy as the defenders of the elderly poor who rely on Medicare and Medicaid. But the Democrats' national decline—or better, their national disintegration—will continue relentlessly and inexorably until they come to grips with these values issues, primarily abortion. I have been saying this for several years. Now, even the president's high-priced pollster, Stanley Greenberg, is saying it: If President Clinton wants to get reelected, advises Greenberg, he must identify with the basic values and economic interests of ordinary Americans. He must become a cultural conservative.

Underlying my electoral calculations was a conviction that the ideas and values I would represent would draw the allegiance of mainstream America. When I put the question, "Who speaks for the child?" I believe that question resonates with the American people. If, as a society, we continue to treat life as something which can be eliminated at will, then what is left? I believe the American people are saying to those who aspire to power, "We care about economic issues, jobs, tax cuts, but we also care about the kind of society we will leave our children. And there is something missing, something fundamentally wrong in America today." That "something" is a moral void, a glorification of the Imperial Self, a world in which everything is relative, where there is no right, no wrong, just a mushy, squishy swamp in which each person is left to wander around defining his or her own personal value system. The results have been chaos and grief. And it's not only left the country reeling from all manner of social dislocation. Now these problems have become very expensive as well.

But even more, I felt I would be a credible messenger for those values because of my life experiences, especially my battle with grave illness. I believed the average person would say, "After all he's been through, he must really believe in what he is saying about the future of the country, and the mission of the Democratic Party. Maybe I should listen to what he has to say."

Viewed in this way, what is perceived as my greatest vulnerability could, at the same time, be my greatest strength.

My brush with death did not "change" me in the sense of suddenly inspiring me to become some kind of messianic messenger, as a few have suggested. No. I was the same person after the experience as before. But in the nearly four years since learning I might die, I had done of lot of thinking. The experience had given me a deeper understanding of myself, of the value of my life and every life. It was hardly a miraculous vision given to me alone. Who has not had such moments? But I was in a position to put it before all America. At the approach of my presidential bid, I felt that maybe I could bring something else to the contest beyond the usual positions and policy ideas and personality clashes over which elections are waged.

I felt at times less like a candidate with an agenda than a witness with a story. I sensed that millions of people across America would respond to my message—because of my own experience with facing death and surviving—as a message somehow purified in the fire of suffering. Not just another message from a politician. Not a Democratic message or a Republican message. Not a message crafted skillfully from polling data or focus groups. Not a message contrived for the purpose of gaining power.

Just a message from one human being who understood vulnerability and suffering, not vicariously but first-hand. A human being who had been on the last rung of the ladder, and was reaching out to all those others on that same rung. A human being who understood what it meant to be powerless, and who, as a result, was better able to use power for the common good. I had walked through an inferno. I had been delivered. What I had seen walking through those flames went beyond all the issues of the day, all the things we so fiercely debated in politics. I wanted to bring that experience and spirit into my campaign. No gloss. No spin. Just that simple. A message offered to the country because of its importance to America's future. A message everyone could understand and feel deep in their own hearts.

I remember one day after my recovery when I had had a similar feeling. It was that horrible evening of Thursday, September 8, 1994, when US Air flight 427 crashed into a field near the Pittsburgh airport. It was in my final months as governor. The next day I went to the scene. All around me, people were running back and forth. Firemen, police officers, medics, nurses, national guardsmen, people from nearby houses who had run to the plane hoping to save the victims. From a helicopter, I surveyed the wreckage. The crash had left a giant, blackened hole in the ground. Strewn across the surrounding area was broken humanity, literally the fragments of human beings who, just minutes before, had been sitting in the comfort of that airliner with thoughts of home and family, jobs and challenges, making plans for tomorrow.

In a CNN interview that night, I tried to express what I felt. I talked about the people of Pennsylvania, and of how this horror had brought out the best in us—the courage and compassion and love of ordinary people. But I walked away from the interview feeling I hadn't really conveyed what was in my heart. I was filled that night, as sometimes during my illness, with a profound sense of human mortality.

In a way, when we look upon such scenes, we are looking truth square in the face. No matter how powerful we may be, or how much we pad our lives with comforts and wealth and the distractions of each day, in the end we are all just frail humanity. Day to day, we don't see it, especially when we're making our way up to those higher rungs of life, when we have power. Even as I write this, now healthy again, I don't feel it as acutely, see it as clearly. But it's true. Those dark moments in a way are the clearest moments of all. They reveal the central fact of our whole existence. We are all vulnerable, all in the end equally powerless. We are powerless when we enter this world and we are powerless when we leave it. In between, we are all pilgrims on the same journey.

Dramatic as my experience had been, in reality it was just an extreme case of what all of us have felt at one time or another. Maybe it's grief or loneliness or unemployment or sickness or just plain failure. Who hasn't been through one of those, when you sit there alone staring life down? Somewhere I have heard the expression, "four-o'clock-in-the-morning courage," and I think I know what it means. All of us do. It's what you need when you wake up in the middle of the night and everything seems completely miserable and dark. I don't mean despair. Just the cold, sober, unaverted gaze at life and death.

Even when we shake the feeling off to rise again for the next day's battle, it remains just as true. We are all pilgrims, winding and curving and coming back again in the same direction; all destined to meet our Maker as we left Him, as powerless and unknowing as children.

From those moments of brokenness often come the first stirrings of real wisdom and strength. And more, real compassion, real love. Once we grasp our own mortality, then life, all life, every life, becomes in our eyes infinitely precious. When we look out upon our fellow man, we don't see strangers anymore. We don't see crowds, or classes, or constituents, or enemies, or voting blocs, or majorities, or minorities. We no longer force human beings into easy categories. Least of all do we draw lines through life, rating "qualities of life," separating the "viable" from the "unviable," or the protected from the unprotected. We love all life. We welcome life because of its very frailty, revere it because of its very helplessness. We throw aside the obstacles and *embrace* it!

This is the only spirit that can ever move us beyond the power-centered arguments in our abortion debate. For me, it renders all such arguments meaningless and hollow. The child is not "viable"? All the more reason to protect it. A child is not yet "complete" or fully developed? Then it is all the more human: we are all "incomplete." The child is imperfect? All the more reason to love it. Whatever it is we have, whatever makes us human, worthy of love and protection, that child has too. Whether a child is viable or unviable, convenient or inconvenient, wanted or unwanted, "defective" or healthy—in that child's heart is the glory of God. Each child—born and unborn—is a heavenly messenger, bearing God's love and hope for all of us.

There are, of course, honest philosophical differences that separate people on the abortion issue. The law is a teacher. Since *Roe* v. *Wade*, a whole generation has grown up in an environment in which abortion has been enshrined as a constitutional right. Given that history, of course there will be profound differences. These are not only understandable, they are inevitable. Most pro-choice people have difficulty with the issue. Many are ambivalent. They defend the practice, but in their hearts understand that something quite serious is involved, something the platitudes and euphemisms of the abortion movement do not quite cover. They tend to rationalize their view by casting abortion as a practical problem. The argument goes something like this: In the best of worlds, we could avoid it. But precisely because people are frail and make mistakes, abortion is necessary. Without it, our problems would be even worse.

In this way, too, I felt myself a witness at the approach of the presidential campaign. Around me in my hospital room, I had seen the best of America—the best doctors, the best technology, the best friends and family a man could hope for. All had rushed to my aid, like angels of mercy, to help a dying man of sixty-one. The most complex medical problems had been solved. The most miraculous technology employed. The most ingenious minds engaged. A women, herself broken and full of sorrow, had saved me.

Down to the very bottom rung, all these hands reached down to pull me back. Why can't we bring the same resources, the same mercy, to helping young mothers and their children? No one can ever persuade me that the situation is hopeless, that we must simply write off the unborn child, that the whole problem is beyond salvaging. I know better. We have the means of salvaging it. I have seen it.

As I neared the campaign decision, I looked back on my whole life and career and medical ordeal. It all seemed to come together in a simple witness for the powerless. This, as best I could deliver it, would be my message: Guiding all political decisions should be an overriding, inviolable respect for our common humanity. No one forgotten. No one counted out. No one left behind. For all our differences we are a family, the human family, and in families all are equally valuable, equally protected, loved, and cared for.

That would be the spirit of my campaign. A concern for those who had been forgotten—working families, the poor, the jobless, the sick, the afflicted, the unborn. Whether it is an eleven-year-old mule boy in the mines with a smashed face and scarred hands; a young black man lying beaten and bloodied; a dying sixty-one-year-old man in need of heroic medical care; or an unwanted, unborn child—what was the difference? We were all vulnerable, all in need of help, all on our way down the same chute, all clinging to the bottom rung.

Every last one of us is important, whether we choose to be or not. All are made in God's own image. Every life is precious. No insignificant person has ever been created. Where the fate of another life is concerned, there is no such thing as a private decision. Everything we do, every moral choice we make, every act of kindness and every act of malice, spreads out into the world bearing a message of hope or despair, and touching in time every life. That one conviction, that all are created equal, has always been the source of America's greatness. Without it, we would all be in serious trouble, and we might not pull through.

I was certain this message would resonate strongly in the cultural debate that would, I believed, be at the center of the 1996 election.

But as that practice session for the 60 *Minutes* interview wore on that day, and then another the next day, and more meetings after that, and fund-raising calls and then travel, mostly with Matt, never-ending travel, another certainty began to settle in: I was tired.

And I knew the reason. Medically, it was not cause for alarm. But I had been taking antibiotics for a sinus infection, and they just seemed to knock me for a loop. The result was deep fatigue. I just couldn't shake it. I kept thinking, "Well, maybe it will pass. Let's see how I feel tomorrow." But when tomorrow came, I felt only more tired.

My luck, it seemed, had finally run out. I seemed to feel the worst just when the 60 *Minutes* filming began at our house in Scranton. On Easter Sunday, it was an effort just to get to church, and then later to the family dinner at Kate's house. I was dragging myself around, fighting a feeling of profound, deadening fatigue. But I couldn't rest.

That Monday we went back again to Pittsburgh, camera crew in tow, for the public event at the hospital to raise public awareness of the urgent need for more organ donors. My visit to the hospital that day was not for any medical reason. But I did not want to leave without saying hello to my doctors. So I met with Dr. Starzl, Dr. Fung, and Dr. Follansbee for a brief social visit. On the way to see them I stopped by to greet the nurses who had taken such good care of me. More filming, and then on to see the doctors while the 60 *Minutes* crew waited just outside the door.

"How are you feeling?" Dr. Starzl asked.

"Not so hot," I said. "I've had this sinus infection for several weeks now. And the antibiotics are really getting to me. No energy. I feel done in all the time. And I've been going around the clock for weeks."

"Are you sure you want to do this?" Starzl asked. "You know, it's been less than two years since the surgery.

"Don't get me wrong," he continued, "If you want to go ahead, we'll certainly back you up. You are making a strong recovery and all the signs are good."

But there was some of the old Starzl enthusiasm missing this time.

Then it was back to the Pittsburgh airport, cameras rolling as we walked through the terminal. A lot of people came up to say hello, offering friendly comments. People were glad to see me, genuinely pleased I was making a strong recovery, and it showed in their faces.

When we got back to Scranton early that evening the producers of 60 *Minutes* went to their hotel, planning to come to our house at 10:00 A.M. the next day for more filming.

As Ellen, Matt, and I rode home that night we talked things over. I was deeply troubled by the possibility that, if I continued, and my stamina down the road was as low as it had been, I would not be able to finish what I'd begun. Meanwhile we would have piled up huge expenditures, raised a great deal of money, and dozens of people would have had to change lives and careers to join the campaign. *How*, I asked myself, *can I ask my friends and supporters to sign up and give their all, if I have doubts about my strength to see it through?* I knew, figuratively speaking, that I could run a 10-K race: I had proved that in my final year as governor. But the question now was whether I was ready for a marathon: a presidential effort requiring almost superhuman energy levels for a protracted period of time.

That night, after another long talk with Ellen and Matt, I made my decision. It all became clear: Another moment of truth, something I just had to face. I was not ready. Not yet. A man going into battle has to feel strong, confident, at the top of his game. I felt weary. Done in. Maybe another day, but not now. It was not to be.

But first we had to go back to Arlington. It was not easy to explain this turn of events to my friends and supporters. They had laid themselves on the line, taken risks. One had even left a well-paying job to join my campaign. He arrived on his first day only to be told I had decided against running. I felt awful about it. But once I'd made the decision, I knew it was the right thing to do—and I have never doubted it since.

"I had to call you together to tell you personally that I've decided not to become a candidate for president," I began. "We were strangers when we first met, and since that time you have helped me in ways I could not expect from my own family. We began this effort convinced we had a message which would attract broad support. I have to say the response has far exceeded even our best expectations. Events have confirmed just how right we were about the power of our message.

"But I've got to be sure, confident, that I have the extraordinary energy to sustain a campaign effort. Today, I have to say I have my doubts. This could change. Months from now, later this year or next, I could feel differently. But, given my current doubts, it's not fair to ask people to give their support.

"It's a terrible disappointment. We're walking away from a vast arsenal. We could have done great things. But now is not the moment. One day, thinking back on it all, we'll understand. We'll know it was the right thing to do."

A press statement had to be drafted. While that was being completed, I called some of our closest friends and most committed supporters to give them the news. Much disappointment, but they all understood. Then I called our press secretary, Karen Walsh, who was in Scranton to work with the producers of 60 *Minutes* at our house that morning. She could hardly believe what I was saying. I asked her to call the producers at their hotel and tell them of my decision. That, I knew, would put the news out on the wires within minutes. About twenty minutes later, CBS reported my decision not to run.

With that, we all parted for awhile. Ellen, Matt, and I walked out to our car and began the long drive back home.

Postscript

GOVERNOR Robert P. Casey finished his second term as Pennsylvania's forty-second governor in January 1995. The Pennsylvania Constitution limits service as governor to two terms.

Governor Casey then became president of Transplant Recipients International (TRIO), an advocacy organization for organ donor recipients, donor families, and those on the waiting list for organs.

In the summer of 1995, he formed two new organizations to place the interests of the family first in the formulation of national policy. One of those, the Campaign for the American Family (CAF), works to change legislation and public policy to help families. The other, the Fund for the American Family (FAF), is an educational foundation whose purpose is to study and report on public issues affecting the family.

Governor Casey is also forming a foundation to raise funds to establish an endowment at the University of Pittsburgh Medical Center to train needy African-American transplant surgeons. The foundation will be named after Michael Lucas, the donor of the heart and liver which saved Casey's life.

Appendices

A New American Compact:

Caring about Women, Caring for the Unborn

EDITORS NOTE: *Following are the text and signatories to a full-page ad that appeared in the* New York Times *during the 1992 Democratic National Convention.*

OVER THE next months and years, the American people will confront again the question that Lincoln posed at Gettysburg: whether a nation conceived in liberty and dedicated to human equality can long endure. In this generation, the issue pressing that question on our consciences is the issue of abortion.

We who propose the new American compact outlined below are men and women of diverse callings and political perspectives. We are public officials, medical professionals, scholars and feminists; we are liberals and conservatives, Democrats, Republicans and Independents, Catholics, Jews, Protestants and agnostics. We have sought to reflect carefully on the abortion controversy. We are making our reflections public in the hope that they will help all Americans cut through the static of the sound bites and discuss the linked questions of abortion, human dignity, and American freedom with the moral seriousness demanded of citizens of a democratic republic.

For almost twenty years, abortion policy in America has been controlled by the courts. That seems likely to remain the case in the immediate future, even though the recent United States Supreme Court decision permits state legislatures to enact some modest regulation of abortion practice. It is to be deeply regretted that the American people have been denied the deliberative role in shaping public policy on this issue that has been played by the citizens of other developed democracies. The American people are capable of serious public moral reflection; the American people are capable of rising above partisanship on a matter of this gravity. Their voice can and must be heard, through the normal procedures of democracy.

For like the practice of slavery, and like the Jim Crow laws of the not-so-distant past, the abortion issue raises the most fundamental questions of justice—questions that cannot be avoided, and that cannot be resolved by judicial fiat. Who belongs to the community of the commonly protected? Whose rights will we acknowledge? Whose human dignity will we respect? For whose well-being will we, as a people, assume responsibility? Profound issues of personal and public morality are engaged by these questions. Their resolution—and the manner in which they are debated—will determine what kind of society America will be in its third century.

A Question of Boundaries

The first two hundred years of the American Republic tell an unfolding tale of aspiration—and progress—toward the ideal of liberty and justice for all. That progress has been rapid in some periods, halting in others; sometimes it has suffered setbacks. But from the early days of the American colonies to our own time, the basic trajectory was consistent and seemingly inexorable. The boundaries of the community of the commonly protected were steadily expanded—and the story of America became the story of an evermore inclusive society. The United States welcomed its immigrants, protected its workers, freed the slaves, enfranchised women, aided the needy, provided social security for the aged, ensured the civil rights of all its citizens and made public spaces accessible to the handicapped: "all in service to its ideals of justice."

Then, in January 1973, the United States Supreme Court, in its *Roe v. Wade* and *Doe v. Bolton* abortion decisions, drastically reversed this pattern of expanding inclusion. In those decisions, seven unelected justices performed the most momentous act of exclusion in our history: they deprived every human being, for the first nine months of his or her life, of the most fundamental human right of all—the right to life.

Let there be no mistake about the impact of the *Roe* and *Doe* decisions: they did not "liberalize" abortion law; they abolished abortion law in all fifty states. Abortion on demand, throughout the full nine months of a pregnancy, for virtually any reason, became public policy in the United States of America. No other developed democracy had, or has, such a permissive abortion regime.

A vast abortion industry, generating some half a billion dollars annually, sprang into existence in the wake of *Roe* and *Doe*. Twenty-five million abortions have been performed in the United States since 1973. Over one and a half million were performed in the past year alone. More than forty percent of those were obtained by women who had already had one or more abortions. But less than five percent of the abortions performed today are performed because of rape, incest, threat to maternal health, or grave fetal deformity. Abortion after *Roe* and *Doe* has become, in the overwhelming majority of cases, a matter of *ex post facto* contraception.

That is not the kind of America that expresses the abiding decency and compassion of our people. It is long past time, we believe, to reconstitute the story of America as a story of inclusion and protection.

Without a Doubt, a Human Life

Those who approve of our current abortion regime sometimes claim that the child in the womb is simply an undifferentiated mass of tissue, an appendage to a woman's body. But modern embryology and fetology exploded such pseudoscience long before *Roe*. Today, the sonogram has given us a veritable window into the womb and has enabled us to observe, in detail, the complex life of the child prior to birth.

From the beginning, each human embryo has its own unique

genetic identity. Three-and-a-half weeks after conception, its heart starts beating. At six weeks, brain activity can be detected. At the end of two months, limbs, fingers, and toes are complete. By three months, the baby is quite active, forming fists, bending arms, and curling toes. At four months, vocal cords, eyelashes, teeth buds, fingernails, and toenails are all present. By five months, the baby is sucking its thumb, punching, kicking, and going through the motions of crying. By six months, it responds to light and sound and can recognize its mother's voice.

Advocates of unrestricted abortion do not want the public to focus on these undeniable facts of fetal development, but the facts cannot be ignored. They make plain that abortion is a violent act, not against "potential life," but against a living, growing human being—a life with potential.

Defending Women's Rights

Abortion is defended today as a means of ensuring the equality and independence of women, and as a solution to the problems of single parenting, child abuse, and the feminization of poverty. The sad truth is that the abortion license has proven to be a disaster for women, children, and families—and, thus, for American society.

We have had virtually unlimited access to abortion for nearly twenty years. Yet during that same period, more and more women and children have slipped into poverty. The insistence, by supporters of abortion on demand, that only "wanted children" be allowed to be born has not improved our infant mortality rates, which have remained among the worst in the industrialized world; nor has it helped us cope effectively with the incidence of child abuse, the frequency and severity of which have increased dramatically during this time.

Unfettered access to abortion on demand has addressed none of women's true needs; nor has it brought dignity to women. It has, in fact, done precisely the opposite. It has encouraged irresponsible or predatory men, who find abortion a convenient justification for their lack of commitment, and has vastly expanded the exploitation of women by the abortion industry. When the United States Supreme Court handed down *Roe* v. *Wade,* it did not even remotely envision the surgical "assembly line," commercialization and exploitation which thousands of women say characterize their experiences with an abortion industry intent on maximizing profits. While apologists for abortion on demand raise the specter of "back alley abortions" in response to virtually any proposed regulation of the abortion industry, the truth is that twenty years of abortion on demand have not eliminated this tragic outcome. Women and young girls still die and are injured by *legally* performed abortions.

We know, now, what happens when society makes the destruction of unborn life a matter of "choice." Mutual, responsible, family planning is de-emphasized. Not only do women experience abortion alone; most relationships fail in its aftermath. The abortion license has not brought freedom and security to women. Rather, it has ushered in a new era of irresponsibility toward women and children, one that now begins before birth. It has retarded the quest for securing women's rights by acting as a cheap substitute for real answers to the injustices women experience today.

Beyond the False Dichotomy; A New Compact of Care

The advocates of abortion on demand falsely assume two things: that women must suffer if the lives of unborn children are legally protected; and that women can only attain equality by having the legal option of destroying their innocent offspring in the womb. The cynicism of these assumptions reflects a terrible failure of moral imagination and social responsibility and an appalling lack of respect for women.

We propose a new understanding, one that does not pit mother against child. To establish justice and to promote the general welfare, America does not need the abortion license. What America needs are policies that responsibly protect and advance the interests of mothers *and* their children, both before *and* after birth. Such policies would provide maximum feasible legal protection for the unborn and maximum feasible care and support for pregnant women, mothers, and children.

Our moral, religious, and political traditions are united in their respect for the dignity of human life. Only in the most extreme circumstances do they permit the taking of life; both our traditions and our law, for example, forbid killing except in cases of legitimate self-defense. And thus, analogously, the laws that protected the unborn prior to *Roe* and *Doe* always contained a "life of the mother" exception. Today, fortunately, pregnancy is very rarely a threat to maternal life or health. Nevertheless, a sound abortion policy would provide for the exceptional case of such a threat by permitting medical procedures necessary to save the life of a pregnant woman even when such procedures would inevitably result in death or injury to her unborn child.

The goal, surely, is an enactment of the most protective laws possible on behalf of the unborn. We recognize that there are disagreements about what is possible and even desirable here. But that is precisely why, as we argued earlier, these issues should be deliberated and decided by the American people according to the democratic processes of persuasion and legislation.

At the same time, a public policy that more adequately expresses the traditions and convictions of the American people will do more than restore legal protection to the unborn.

It will take seriously the needs of women whose social or economic circumstances might tempt them to seek the abortion "solution." It will recognize our shared responsibility, in public and private settings, to make realistic alternatives to abortion available to such women. It will support women in caring for the children they choose to raise themselves, and it will help them find homes for those they cannot raise. It will work to provide a decent life for mother and child before and *after* birth.

In sum, we can and we must adopt solutions that reflect the dignity and worth of every human being and that embody understanding of the community's shared responsibility for creating policies that are truly pro-woman *and* pro-child. What we seek are communities and policies that help women to deal with crisis pregnancies by eliminating the crisis, not the child.

Common Choices, Common Destiny

The rhetoric of abortion advocacy contains a truth that abortion advocates often fail to perceive. Abortion *is* a question of choice. The "choice," though, is not one faced by isolated women exercising private rights. It is a choice faced by all the citizens of this free society. And the choice we make, deliberatively and democratically, will do much to answer two questions: What kind of a people are we? What kind of a people will we be?

If we abandon the principle of respect for human life by making the value of life depend on whether someone else thinks that life is worthy or wanted, we will become one sort of people.

But there is a better way.

We can choose to reaffirm our respect for human life. We can choose to extend once again the mantle of protection to all members of the human family, including the unborn. We can choose to provide effective care for mothers and children.

And if we make those choices, America will experience a new birth of freedom, bringing within it a renewed spirit of community, compassion and caring.

[The names and affiliations of the signatories follow.]

ROBERT P. CASEY
GOVERNOR
COMMONWEALTH OF PENNSYLVANIA

HUGH L. CAREY
FORMER GOVERNOR
STATE OF NEW YORK

PETER S. LYNCH
BOSTON, MASSACHUSETTS

CAROLYN A. LYNCH
BOSTON, MASSACHUSETTS

MARY CUNNINGHAM AGEE
EXECUTIVE DIRECTOR AND FOUNDER
THE NURTURING NETWORK
BOISE, IDAHO

HADLEY ARKES, PH.D.
PROFESSOR OF AMERICAN INSTITUTIONS
AMHERST COLLEGE
AMHERST, MASSACHUSETTS

MARC GELLMAN, PH.D.
CHAIRMAN, MEDICAL ETHICS COMMITTEE
  OF THE U.J.A. FEDERATION
DIX HILLS, NEW YORK

PASTOR E. JEAN THOMPSON, D.D.
PRESIDENT
INTERNATIONAL BLACK WOMEN'S NETWORK
WASHINGTON, D.C.

JAMES KURTH, PH.D.
SWARTHMORE COLLEGE
SWARTHMORE, PENNSYLVANIA

EUNICE KENNEDY SHRIVER
POTOMAC, MARYLAND

SARGENT SHRIVER
POTOMAC, MARYLAND

JEANNIE WALLACE FRENCH, M.P.H.
FOUNDER AND DIRECTOR
NATIONAL WOMEN'S COALITION FOR LIFE
ALEXANDRIA, VIRGINIA

WILLIAM E. SIMON
MORRISTOWN, NEW JERSEY

J. F. DONAHUE FAMILY
PITTSBURGH, PENNSYLVANIA

MOSHE TENDLER, PH.D.
PROFESSOR OF BIBLICAL LAW
   AND MEDICAL ETHICS
YESHIVA UNIVERSITY
NEW YORK, NEW YORK

DAVID NOVAK, PH.D.
EDGAR M. BRONFMAN PROFESSOR OF
   MODERN JUDAIC STUDIES
UNIVERSITY OF VIRGINIA
CHARLOTTESVILLE, VIRGINIA

WILLIAM C. PORTH, JR., ESQUIRE
CHARLESTON, WEST VIRGINIA

GEORGE WEIGEL
PRESIDENT
ETHICS AND PUBLIC POLICY CENTER
WASHINGTON, D.C.

MARY ANN GLENDON
HARVARD UNIVERSITY SCHOOL OF LAW
CAMBRIDGE, MASSACHUSETTS

SIDNEY CALLAHAN, PH.D.
MERCY COLLEGE
DOBBS FERRY, NEW YORK

PATRICIA WESLEY, M.D.
YALE UNIVERSITY SCHOOL OF MEDICINE
NEW HAVEN, CONNECTICUT

RONALD J. SIDER, PH.D.
EVANGELICALS FOR SOCIAL ACTION
PHILADELPHIA, PENNSYLVANIA

MICHAEL MCCONNELL
UNIVERSITY OF CHICAGO LAW SCHOOL
CHICAGO, ILLINOIS

IRENE ESTEVES
NATIONAL DIRECTOR
PROFESSIONAL WOMEN'S NETWORK
CHICAGO, ILLINOIS

JON LEVENSON, PH.D.
ALBERT LIST PROFESSOR OF JEWISH STUDIES
HARVARD UNIVERSITY
CAMBRIDGE, MASSACHUSETTS

RACHEL MACNAIR, PRESIDENT
FEMINISTS FOR LIFE OF AMERICA
KANSAS CITY, MISSOURI

LEON R. KASS, M.D.
UNIVERSITY OF CHICAGO
CHICAGO, ILLINOIS

NAT HENTOFF
NEW YORK, NEW YORK

CHRISTINE SMITH TORRE, ESQUIRE
EXECUTIVE DIRECTOR
FEMINISTS FOR LIFE LAW PROJECT
WOODLYN, PENNSYLVANIA

ROBERT P. GEORGE, PH.D.
PRINCETON UNIVERSITY
PRINCETON, NEW JERSEY

KATHY WALKER
PRESIDENT
WOMEN EXPLOITED BY ABORTION, INC.
VENUS, TEXAS

PROFESSOR GERARD V. BRADLEY
NOTRE DAME LAW SCHOOL
NOTRE DAME, INDIANA

THE REVEREND RICHARD JOHN NEUHAUS
PRESIDENT
INSTITUTE ON RELIGION AND PUBLIC LIFE
NEW YORK, NEW YORK

MICHELINE MATHEWS-ROTH, M.D.
HARVARD MEDICAL SCHOOL
BOSTON, MASSACHUSETTS

EDMUND D. PELLEGRINO, M.D.
JOHN CARROLL PROFESSOR OF MEDICINE
   AND MEDICAL ETHICS
GEORGETOWN UNIVERSITY
WASHINGTON, D.C.

REMARKS BY GOVERNOR ROBERT P. CASEY

DELIVERED AT THE FORTY-SEVENTH ANNUAL DINNER OF

THE ALFRED E. SMITH MEMORIAL FOUNDATION, INC.

WALDORF-ASTORIA HOTEL, NEW YORK CITY

—THURSDAY, OCTOBER 15, 1992

YOUR EMINENCE, Cardinal O'Connor, Governor Carey, Mayor Dinkins, Senator Moynihan, Senator D'Amato, Attorney General Abrams, Al Smith, members of the clergy, distinguished guests, ladies and gentlemen.

I am most grateful to you, Your Eminence, for your kind words and generous invitation to be here tonight. And I salute you for your powerful witness and the great work you are doing here in the Archdiocese of New York to help the most vulnerable and needy members of the family of New York.

Now, it's no secret that I'm a last-minute substitute here tonight. Traditionally, this dinner has featured the presidential candidates. But tonight's debate got in the way.

Does it bother me to play second fiddle, you ask? To be second choice? Not on your life.

Politicians do it all the time.

We love to finish second.

Let me tell you how it happened.

Several months ago, Al Smith called to invite me to speak at tonight's dinner.

He was kind of hesitant, and finally acknowledged that I was to be a back-up speaker, in the event the presidential candidates were unavailable.

I said, "Al, that's fine. No problem!"

Some time later, Al called again and said, "Governor, the presidential candidates are coming, and you're relieved. Thanks a lot, but we won't need you after all."

I said, "Al, that's fine. Glad to be of help."

Shortly thereafter, Al called again and said, "Governor, you're on again. The presidential candidates are debating the night of the dinner and won't be able to make it."

I said, "Al, that's fine. No problem."

Two weeks later, Al called again and said, "Governor, the presidential debate has been scheduled for 9:00 P.M., and we are cutting back on the program. You'll have to cut your speech from twenty minutes to ten minutes. And I've got to warn you. If you go beyond ten minutes, the Cardinal will give you the hook."

. . ."Al, that's fine."

A few days ago, Al called again and said, "It turns out that the play-off between the Blue Jays and the Athletics may conflict with our dinner; so you're going to have to cut your speech from ten minutes to five minutes."

To myself I said, "Hey Al, who do you think you're talking to, Rodney Dangerfield?"

But to Al I said, "Al, that's fine. But I have a counter offer. I'll write the speech. It'll be two-and-a-half minutes long. And do me a favor, save me the bus fare to New York. I'll fax you the speech, and you can read it—during the seventh-inning stretch of the ballgame between the Blue Jays and the A's."

But thanks to the Blue Jays, there was no seventh game. So here I am.

After that harrowing experience, I almost feel like echoing those memorable words of Admiral Stockdale in the vice presidential debate when he said, "Who am I? And what am I doing here?"

But politicians get put down all the time. It's good for our humility. The first rule in this business is never take yourself too seriously.

I was running for re-election in 1990 as an incumbent Governor. It was just before the election. Going down the home stretch. Campaigning in Oil City, a small town in western Pennsylvania, walked up to a fellow in a gas station and asked for his vote. He said, "I've heard of you. As a matter of fact, I've decided to vote for you."

I asked him why.

He said, "Because anybody would be better than the guy that's in there now."

So if you think you're a big deal, take a ride to Oil City, Pennsylvania.

But the real reason I'm here tonight is because I knew Cardinal O'Connor when he was Bishop of Scranton. Many people here tonight have asked me what he was like in those days.

And I told them he was very soft-spoken and retiring, shied away from controversy, and never got in the paper—and I'm certain that New York City hasn't changed him a bit.

I AM profoundly honored to be here tonight—and I cannot help thinking of my father, who went to work in the anthracite coal mines of Pennsylvania when he was eleven years old, earned his high school diploma in his late twenties, never went to college, and then became a lawyer at the age of forty after working his way through Fordham Law School.

I was born in Queens—and I still believe that my real claim to fame is that the doctor who delivered me was Jimmy Cagney's brother.

My father loved New York. And Al Smith was one of his heroes. Largely because of my father, this city has always held a special fascination and attraction for me. Call it roots. Call it what you will. But the bond is strong. And it's in my bones.

We returned often when I was young, and I learned the sidewalks of Al Smith's New York. And my father's values—values I learned to admire and respect—were the values of Al Smith—integrity, caring for those less fortunate, fierce loyalty to family, strong faith.

That, above all, is what this dinner is all about.

Not just help for those in need, as important as that is.

Not just honor to the memory of a great man, as worthy as he may have been.

But a commitment to witness and work for a society equal to the defining legacy of Al Smith.

To this day, he remains a powerful summons to a great and continuing challenge—to advance the tolerance which his life embodied, his presidential nomination vindicated, and his shameful defeat denied.

I BELIEVE tolerance is once again at risk—in a different way than it was then, but one that also goes to the heart and the summit of our public life.

The immediate cause is the issue of abortion—and this time the danger comes from a political tradition from which I myself come. There is a new liberal intolerance which will not abide doubt or dissent—which claims it stands for freedom of choice, but stifles freedom of speech. And so a movement which began by saying let every person decide, has ended up by trying to silence anyone who disagrees—whether at a lock-step national convention, or in a disrupted public forum at Cooper Union or in media that seem to be mostly of a single mind.

Thus, I'm told that the television networks refused to run the ads created by the Arthur S. DeMoss Foundation—ads which do not call for outlawing abortion, but only seek to persuade individuals to decide against it—"Life. What a beautiful choice." Are we now to be told not even to appeal to individual conscience?

This absolutism, the imposed conformity which treats the right to life as an idea beyond even the pale of discussion, has peer and precedent in our national history. In 1860, at Cooper Union, Lincoln warned of an established opinion which would tolerate nothing short of saying slavery is right—which "will grant a hearing to pirates or to murderers" but not to opponents of slavery. Are we now to tolerate, in whole segments of our society, on campuses, in most mainstream journals, in great political conventions, only those who agree to say abortion is right?

I DO NOT say any of this in a spirit of confrontation. My intention is the opposite. I know there are some at this dinner who surely disagree on the substance of the abortion issue. I respect their view; I ask only that they respect the view I share with so many others. I ask only that those who believe in the right to life be accorded the right to speak.

To my own party, I would say simply: Why is the position on this issue taken by numerous Democratic congressmen, and elected Democrats at all levels of government across this country, who all oppose abortion, now so unacceptable that it must be unspoken among us?

Do we not have the right—I would say the duty—to advocate reasonable measures such as parental consent and a waiting period—measures supported by a vast majority of the American people?

DO WE not have the right to argue and persuade and attempt to move people farther in the direction we believe our country ought to go? Is this not the essence of democracy?

And do we not have the duty, those of us who believe in the right to life, to defend it not just until birth, but afterwards—by working to improve the lives women and children will lead, by health care and child nutrition and other measures of social justice? Do we not have to examine our own consciences according to this standard?

These are moral issues—and I believe they can and should be weighed in those terms, not dealt with on the basis of religious labels or stereotypes. There are millions who oppose abortion who are not Catholic; people of all faiths; people of no faith.

This is not a question of church and state, but of conscience and state—and in my view, it must be freely debated.

There is an indefensible contradiction between liberal principles as I once learned them and the new liberal intolerance. There are also disturbing signs that the intolerance has reached beyond the issue of abortion to religious belief itself—bringing us in a sad full circle back to the 1928 of Al Smith.

Let me count some of the ways: suggestions appear in the press that a Supreme Court nominee should be examined more closely than usual because he was once Catholic. A group at the Democratic National Convention, opposed to my right to life position, hands out buttons showing me dressed as the Pope. A rock singer rips the Pope's picture to pieces on national television. And the Host is thrown to the ground and trampled by a protester in Saint Patrick's Cathedral.

Anti-Catholicism has become a fashionable, barely disguised prejudice. A cancer in our national life every bit as malignant as racism or anti-Semitism. The legacy of the man whose memory we revere tonight would be dishonored if we were to fail to condemn all such forms of bigotry and hatred. And to tear them out by the roots, wherever we find them in our society.

SO MY plea tonight is that we respect each other. That whatever the strength of our feelings—and on abortion, mine, as many of you know, are very strong—let us at least give each other a hearing, debate the merits and refuse to indulge appeals to bigotry, suspicion or stereotype.

If we set that standard, on this issue and every other, in discussions and elections on every level, then this country will become a more tolerant place.

Let us remember, tonight and always, what poisoned so much of America against Al Smith—and let us honor and fulfill for our country the ideals which Al Smith did so much to advance.

COMMENCEMENT ADDRESS BY

GOVERNOR ROBERT P. CASEY

TO THE FRANCISCAN UNIVERSITY OF

STEUBENVILLE

STEUBENVILLE, OHIO

—MAY 14, 1994

THANK YOU. President [Michael] Scanlan, Father Jordan [Hite], chairman of the board of trustees, members of the board, Sister Margaret [Carney], Father John Catoir, Dean [Michael] Healy, members of the faculty—I'm very honored to join you here today.

To the graduating class of 1994: my congratulations.

My wife Ellen and I are the veterans of eight undergraduate commencement exercises—twelve, if you throw in graduate degrees. Our last is scheduled for May of 1997 at Georgetown Law School. So let me begin with a salute to all my fellow parents here today.

I'm grateful and honored to be here.

MANY of the commencement speeches I've heard or read over the years have been, frankly, pretty depressing. These speeches are generally an occasion for warning: assessments of how the world is shaping up, of dangers to be guarded against, of ominous developments to be watched.

Last year, for instance, graduates in Austin, Texas, heard America's problems described as a "crisis of meaning." The call went out for a Politics of Meaning. Another audience in Washington recently heard a very powerful speech about, as the speaker put it, America's "turning away of the soul." In one case the speaker was Hillary Clinton. In the other case, former Education Secretary William J. Bennett.

Although the terms are similar, no doubt in the details they mean quite different things. But it tells us something interesting that they and others strike the same theme. It's probably fair to say that America is slowly arriving at a rough consensus. We are at last beginning to realize that there are problems beyond the power of politics or science or wealth to repair. More and more we sense an absence. A void. We seem to agree that something crucial is missing from what, by all material calculations, should be the picture of perfect national contentment.

Surveying this scene, it may be that we are passing through our own American version of "Darkness at Noon." Just when we have prevailed in the "long, twilight struggle," we find ourselves in domestic quarrels more and more bitter. In a country founded on ideas of opportunity and community and generosity, we find ourselves locked in often frenzied quarrels over who gets what; whose rights come first and whose last; and even who gets to live and who doesn't.

Just as the economic cycle comes around again to lift us up, promising greater wealth and security, we find more and more homes falling apart.

A society with more lawyers than any other and the oldest surviving constitution, we are the most lawless in the world; the freest of nations, yet also the most violent. You are safer today walking the streets of Belfast or Hebron than you are in parts of some of our cities.

And even more bizarre, as you walk our cities you can even find popular music and art celebrating that very brutality, reveling in it. Indeed, if one word sums up whatever it is that troubles the American soul, that would be it right there: violence. In speeches we describe the crisis in very lofty, philosophical language, but at the end of the day that seems to be what we have — a violent streak.

To this list of American traits I would add only one point. At the same time, we are a culture of staggering generosity, heroic self-sacrifice, and envied brilliance. We could cite all kinds of evidence for this—the tens of billions Americans give to charities, our foreign aid, the work of our churches, our social services both public and private. But I say this as someone who in the last year has witnessed all three qualities up close, from that unique view of life afforded from a hospital room. From that seat of powerlessness, I saw that other America we celebrate in our more hopeful moments. The "compassionate" America my party used to talk about and believe in: a society of caring, healing, heroism, resolve, bold endeavor, brotherhood.

Just a few weeks ago the papers reported a new breakthrough in the treatment of fatal diseases through gene alteration. Think of the good this might bring, the suffering it might spare. Where else but in America is such a project even conceivable? And who, in the face of such possibilities, can even guess how things will look one day when you're attending the graduations of your own children?

Viewing the whole picture, though, there is just no getting around the violent streak. Our capacity for creativity seems at times to be overtaken only by our capacity for destruction. Sometimes the violence is so aggressive that the hospitals and homes and campuses like this come to seem like small fortresses, places of refuge. In some respects our culture resembles a place foreseen by the Scottish author John Buchan. Writing fifty years ago, he described "the coming of a too garish age, when life would be lived in the glare of neon lamps and the spirit would have no solitude."

In such a world, he said:

> . . . everyone would have leisure. But everyone would be restless, for there would be no spiritual discipline in life. . . . It would be a feverish, bustling world, self-satisfied and yet malcontent, and under the mask of a riotous life there would be death at the heart. In the perpetual hurry of life there would be no quiet for the soul. [In such a world] life would be rationalized and padded with every material comfort, [but] there would be little satisfaction for the immortal part of man.

Along with Mrs. Clinton and Mr. Bennett, different observers come forward with different explanations for the situation. Some make the familiar point that learning and technology run inevitably at an unequal pace; that in the race of progress, wisdom and goodness will always lag behind power. Others believe it arises from uniquely American vices; they say it's the ruthless underside of our culture of contentment and self-gratification. Still others, like the first lady, offer a vaguely spiritual diagnosis.

But whatever explanation we favor, I am absolutely sure of one thing. And I offer it as my contribution to the national debate. There is nothing at all vague about our problems. They are not of some mysterious origin. All people in all times have suffered from vague spiritual anxieties, and we should not expect to be any different. In the end, our national griefs are of our own making. They arise from decisions we have made, and have it in our power to reverse. They come from evils we have invited, and may yet banish. They are the fruit of acts of violence we have permitted—and in some quarters even celebrated.

And I am just as sure of this. All of these trends, these disturbing, violent, garish trends, come together in the issue of abortion. Whatever fine gloss we put on it, here is the ultimate act of unreason, of aggression, of exploitation of the weak by the strong. Because abortion is the ultimate violence. The abortion movement isn't just another cause; it is the telltale passion of a deeply disturbed society.

The clearest evidence of this is the yearning among those who defend abortion to put the issue behind us, their gnawing anxiety to put it all out of their minds, to make us all forget it and move on. Other ages knew this tragedy, but they at least saw it as tragedy. Ours alone has dared to call it a good. We alone have dared to call the victim a "thing," the act a "service," the killer a "provider."

We have spent a generation constructing a world in which unborn babies are but expendable tissue, this make-believe world of death without tears—and then we wonder why our culture is so violent! We permit the casual destruction of the most meaningful thing on earth at a rate of 1.6 million a year—and then wonder why our own lives seem to hold so little meaning. Should we really be surprised that in such a society life comes to seem cheaper and cheaper? Is a happy, healthy abortion culture even imaginable? Other ages had abortion, but our age lives with something more on its conscience. We've made not only a right of abortion, but a lucrative industry. And what decent society can live peacefully with that?

BUT THAT is only part of my message. The other side of it is this. In the long term, our cultural unease with abortion, this refusal to drop the subject, is our most hopeful sign of health. Other countries, sadly, have more or less learned to live with it; they don't see it as anything to get worked up about. But not here. This thing—this horrible thing so contrary to our ideals, our inclusiveness, our kindness, our love for one another—has been grafted onto American society. But it is not a functioning organ—it's a disfigurement. It won't take. It won't heal. The body rejects it.

Think, for example, of the memorial you have here to the unborn child. When I saw it this morning, I thought two things.

First, I thought how beautiful it is that young people like you can share in such a memorial. We're always hearing of the "new generation" with its proud, matter-of-fact, unapologetic embrace of the abortion culture. But as that "herd of independent minds" on other campuses charges onward, grows more and more militant and gullible, here there is still enough calm to see the tragedy of it all; to refuse enlistment in such a cause. It must be very hard sometimes to hold to your conscience in such a culture. You face pressures that in my youth we never knew. I am honored to be in the presence of young people who have the courage and integrity to do that.

But then, looking down at the memorial, I thought something else. I couldn't help but imagine what would happen if a monument like that appeared on any other campus. Just imagine the rage, the bitterness, the resentment! What we see as a beautiful and humane symbol, an expression of our brotherhood with all humanity, others would greet as an outrageous, intolerable provocation. Such a symbol would not last a day without being encircled by an angry mob demanding its prompt removal.

I believe the reason for all that anger is very simple. In looking at such reminders, we look at ourselves, at our whole country and its purpose. We on the pro-life side are always faulted for our curious "obsession" with the subject, but really, it's the others who cannot quite let it go. Theirs is the obsession of people in denial, furiously repressing all doubts, hiding all the troubling details, hating any who would disturb their moral slumber.

The abortion issue has that effect on people: It forces you to decide who you are, how you live, what life itself is all about. When all the shouting matches and tortuous arguments are over, when all the heated marches and rallies are disbanded, here in the end is what they cannot face: a tiny grave. And in a way, you can't blame them for their anger: Who in their position would not be pained? What ardent abortion activist could look down at that, and in the quiet of his or her heart affirm, "Yes, this is what I believe in. I can live with this?"

That memorial here on campus—I suppose at times it must seem to you a lonely, forlorn symbol, a solitary gesture in a forgotten, hopeless cause. But today I want to offer a much more encouraging report. I don't believe for one moment that it is a forgotten cause. The abortion movement is doomed to fail; it is a crusade without a cross. Quietly, slowly, painfully, America is facing up to these questions. Is this really what we want? Is *this* the endpoint of progress? Is this the sort of culture we want our own children to live in? Must we really destroy what we lack the courage to love? And America's answer, the more we are pressed with the issue, is No.

If anyone doubts this, here's a question for you: Remember the Freedom of Choice Act? I seem to recall that this legislation was going to enshrine, once and for all, the holdings of *Roe* v. *Wade*. It was to be the culmination of the whole abortion movement.

But when last seen, it was being quietly tabled for later consideration. In other words, it failed. It didn't have the votes. Here we have a presidency, a House, and a Senate controlled by the party formally committed to unrestricted abortion. We have in such groups as NARAL and Planned Parenthood perhaps the most ferocious, relentless lobby in Washington. And yet, in the end, they were afraid even to bring their bill to the floor. After all the big talk and bold promises, they couldn't pull it off. Neither, it turns out, could they repeal the Hyde Amendment.

And this year, a good number of states, including Pennsylvania, have refused to comply with the recent White House edict requiring states to disregard state restrictions on public funding of abortions in the cases of rape and incest.

And on other fronts, the abortion movement continues to wane. Consider this fact reported a year ago in *USA Today*:

> Despite President Clinton's reversal of a ban on abortions at military hospitals overseas, . . . no U.S. military doctors will perform abortions. The Pentagon confirmed Wednesday that all forty-four military doctors in Europe have decided against doing the procedure on moral and religious grounds.

And then there was the *Wall Street Journal* article reporting on a study of medical schools at Columbia and the University of California at Davis. The study found a sharp decline in the number of medical schools offering abortion training, as well as the number of students even willing to take such courses.

Listen to Dr. Trent MacKay, the author of the study: "There is certainly a stigma attached to it now. In many communities it is not an acceptable thing to do. . . ." Moreover, the story reports, "even those medical schools who offer training are running into another problem—the absence of mentors willing to set themselves up as role models." Dr. MacKay calls this "the graying of the abortion provider."

And finally, consider the remarkable sight we witnessed on television after Mother Teresa's recent appearance in Washington. She was there to speak at a prayer breakfast. To her right sat the president of the United States and his wife. To her left, the vice president of the United States and his wife.

Said Mother Teresa, "Any country that accepts abortion is not teaching its people to love, but to use any violence to get what they want. This is why the greatest destroyer of love and peace is abortion."

"Many people," Mother Teresa continued, "are very, very concerned with the children of India, with the children of Africa, where quite a few die of hunger, and so on. Many people are also concerned with all the violence in this great country of the United States. These concerns are very good. But often these same people are not concerned with the millions who are being killed by the deliberate decisions of their mothers. And this is what is the greatest destroyer of peace today—abortion, which brings people to such blindness."

Well, if every age is remembered by a snapshot image, one picture that captures something essential about the times, here was a new one for the gallery. Saying these words, Mother Teresa was almost drowned out in applause. Everybody applauded, except four people. And as one who has spent a lot of energy pursuing political power myself, I had to wonder: What power is really worth the price of having to sit in the presence of someone like that, and hear her message in awkward silence? What have we come to when the leaders of the free world are not even free to applaud words of such obvious wisdom and power?

But despite that sad image, we continue to hope. Men are complex, and despite all pressures may yet find the strength of truth within themselves. It was only a year ago, and not far from here, that, in Chillicothe, Ohio, President Clinton put it this way.

"Very few Americans," he said, "believe that all abortions, all the time, are all right. Almost all Americans believe abortions should be illegal when the children can live without the mother's assistance, when the children can live outside the mother's womb."

By referring to the unborn as children, the president was not making a theological claim, or even a controversial claim. He was just saying what we all know by instinct, common sense, and conscience. It was an unguarded moment. This is how a man sounds when he is letting his heart speak, without regard to political pressures or ideological etiquette.

In a less vivid way, similar pressures will always confront each one of us, and especially each of you as you leave today on your different journeys. However complex the situation, however great the pressures, always the challenge will be the same: to weigh the real value of things.

The world will try again and again, in a thousand different forms, to sell you power, popularity, acceptance. But look very closely because usually the price is a high one. The price is to surrender the greatest power and freedom any man or woman could ever have—your conscience.

Let me send you off with this thought. In past ages, a person looking for the world's centers of power would have pointed to some government temple or tribune or emperor. Never, 1,500 years ago, would anyone ever have thought to look for power and influence in a dark cave in Assisi. I believe something similar can be said of our world. At times in life you will feel weak, vulnerable, outnumbered. So did St. Francis. And yet he was never discouraged. Despite all odds, he pressed on. And today those great powers, built by force, have fallen by force. They have long since rotted away, while the work of St. Francis lives on in you.

This is the message I leave with you: Never forget that beneath all the slogans and fierce arguments is the fate of innocent children. They need your love; their mothers need your courage. Do not be discouraged in the face of scorn: Press on!

Try, as St. Francis and all the really great ones have done, to have compassion for those who offer only anger and bitterness. In the long term, you possess no greater weapon: Press on!

And finally, give your country not what it wants or will reward, but what it needs. Lend it in your own lives that goodness without which it cannot be great, and the grace without which it cannot be saved: Press on!

ALL OF US are joined in our conviction that abortion is a bad thing. And although many of us are Catholics, we are also joined in the conviction that abortion is not simply a Catholic concern. It's a catholic concern with the small "c"—the concern of anyone who rejects the idea of human life as a disposable commodity. The concern of anyone with eyes to see, a mind to reason, and a heart to feel.

It is not an arrogant boast, but a demographic fact, that most Americans share this conviction. Anytime the question is put squarely to them, "Do you oppose abortion on demand?" more than two out of three Americans answer yes. Asked if they favor restrictions on abortion such as we have enacted in Pennsylvania, again a majority of 70 to 80 percent say yes. Perhaps the most telling survey of all found that 78 percent of the people would outlaw 93 percent of all abortions—all but the familiar hard cases. Even in the last election, in which all sides sought to shelve the issue of abortion, exit polls revealed its central importance in the minds of most voters.

[247]

To those who favor liberal abortion policies, this persistent opposition is a mystery, a disturbing sign of something backward and intolerant in our society. Sometimes the abortion lobby pretty much concedes that Americans by and large favor restrictions on abortion—as when Pennsylvania's abortion laws were upheld by the Supreme Court. Such setbacks to their cause leave abortion advocates bewildered and alarmed, convinced that Americans still need to be "educated on the issue."

Other times—like right now—their tactic is to obscure public opinion by marginalizing the pro-life side, dismissing critics of their cause as a handful of fanatics resisting the tide of opinion. A quarter of a million people may gather to protest abortion on the Washington Mall, and if the media notice them at all, they're treated almost in a tone of pity, like some narrow fringe estranged from modern realities. As I discovered, even the governor of a major state, who holds pro-life views, can be denied a hearing at his party's convention without the national media protesting it. The success of this tactic is truly a public relations triumph, only possible in an environment which constantly marginalizes and suppresses the pro-life message. And despite twenty years of brainwashing, the American people have not been fooled. If the majority of Americans support abortion, why have three of the last four presidential elections been won resoundingly by pro-life candidates? If my position is irrelevant, then so, I'm afraid, are the views of some 80 to 85 percent of the people of Pennsylvania and the United States.

As I read the polls showing our continuing unease with abortion, nothing makes me more proud to call myself an American. Among the "herd of independent minds" who make up our opinion leaders, abortion may be taken as a mark of progress. But most Americans have not followed. In the abortion lobby's strange sense of the word, America has never been a "progressive" nation. For we know—and this used to be the credo of my party—that progress can never come by exploiting or sacrificing any one class of people. Progress is a hollow word unless everyone is counted in and no one written off, especially the most weak and vulnerable among us.

You cannot stifle this debate with a piece of paper. No edict, no federal mandate can put to rest the grave doubts of the American people.

Legal abortion will never rest easy on this nation's conscience. It will continue to haunt the consciences of men and women everywhere. The plain facts of biology, the profound appeals of the heart, are far too unsettling to ever fade away.

THE QUESTION I want to address tonight, then, is this: What are the responsibilities of a pro-life politician?

For no matter what the majority sentiments may be, the drift of law favors abortion. Our courts, which do not operate on majority rule, say abortion is legal, an implied constitutional right to privacy found nowhere in the text of the Constitution. For a politician like myself, opposition to abortion may thus become opposition to the existing laws one is sworn to uphold.

What then do conscience and duty require?

I believe the first step is to understand that such dilemmas are not new to our day. Any man who has ever tried to use political power for the common good has felt an awful sense of powerlessness. There are always limits on what we can do, always obstacles, always frustrations and bitter disappointments. This was the drama a future president once studied in *Profiles in Courage*, a book that now seems quaint in its simple moral idealism. The founders of our country understood the limits of political power when they swore allegiance to something higher, their "sacred honor." Lincoln felt this tension when he sought to uphold the equality of men. His real greatness was in seeing that political reform alone wasn't enough; not only the slave had to be freed, but the slave owner from the bonds of his own moral blindness. Likewise, Thomas More expressed the dilemma when, faced with the raw power of the state, he declared, "I die the king's good servant but God's first." Far from being a new problem, this tension goes all the way back to the Pharisees and their challenge to declare for or against Caesar.

Just as the problem is an old one, so are the alternatives. One of these alternatives is accommodation with power, a pragmatic acceptance of "the facts." In the abortion question, this position is summed up in familiar disavowal, "I'm personally opposed, but . . ."

The hard facts—so runs this view—are against us. However we might oppose it, abortion is a sad feature of modern life. Tolerance is the price we pay for living in a free, pluralistic society. For the Catholic politician to "impose" his moral views would be an act of theocratic arrogance, violating our democratic trust. The proper and prudent course is therefore to bring change by "persuasion, not coercion." Absent a "consensus," it is not the place of any politician to change our laws permitting abortion.

I want to be careful here not to caricature this position. Some very honorable people hold it, and it is not my purpose to challenge their motives. Yet, as some politicians advance this view it does seem an evasion, a finesse rather than an honest argument. But that, so far as I am concerned, is the secret of their own individual hearts. Here I mean only to challenge the argument on its own intellectual grounds, with the presumption of good faith extended all around.

We can dispense easily with the charge of theocratic arrogance. That would certainly apply if we were trying to impose some uniquely Catholic stricture like church attendance or fast days on the general population. But the stricture to refrain from killing is not uniquely Catholic. And that, as a purely empirical assertion, is how nearly all people of all faiths at all times have regarded abortion—as killing. Just listen, for example, to Frank Sussman, the lawyer who represented Missouri abortion clinics in *Webster*.

"Neither side in this debate"—he said—"would ever disagree on the physiological facts. Both sides would agree as to when a heartbeat can first be detected. Both sides would agree as to when brain waves can first be detected. But when you try to place the emotional labels on what you call that collection of physiological facts, that is where people part company."

Or listen to former New York Mayor Ed Koch, a fellow Democrat: "I support *Roe* v. *Wade* wholeheartedly," he wrote in a column. "And I do it even while acknowledging to myself that at some point, perhaps even after the first trimester, abortion becomes infanticide. . . ."

Or, for that matter, just listen to President Clinton speaking last month in Chillicothe, Ohio: "Very few Americans believe that all abortions all the time are all right. Almost all Americans believe that abortions should be illegal when the children can live without the mother's assistance, when the children can live outside the mother's womb."

By referring to the unborn as "children," the president was not making a theological claim; he was just putting all the physiological facts together. The same is true when we say abortion "kills." We don't say it in meanness. It's a unique kind of killing, for the motive may not be homicidal; it may be done in ignorance of what actually is occurring. We reserve a special compassion for women who find themselves contemplating abortion. But as an objective fact, that is what abortion is, and so mankind has always regarded it. Science, history, philosophy, religion, and common intuition all speak with one voice in asserting the humanity of the unborn. Only our current laws say otherwise.

So much for theocratic arrogance. That is the more obvious fallacy underlying the "personally opposed, but . . ." line of reasoning.

But I believe it arises from a deeper intellectual confusion. It confuses prudence with pragmatism, and mistakes power for authority.

Prudence we all know to be a virtue. Classical thinkers rated it the supreme political virtue. Roughly defined, it's the ability to distinguish the desirable from the possible. It's a sense of the good, joined with a practical knowledge of the means by which to accomplish the good. A world in which every unborn child survives to take his first breath is desirable. But we know that such a world has never been. And prudence cautions us never to expect such a world. Abortion is but one of many evils that, to one extent or another, is to be found at all times and places. Men can make good laws, but laws cannot make men good.

But the point is that after facing up to such facts, the basic facts of our human condition, prudence does not fall silent. It is not an attitude of noble resignation; it is an active virtue. The voice that says, "Ah, well, there is no consensus. We must take the world as it is. There is nothing further to be done"—that is not the voice of prudence. It is the voice of expediency.

Prudence compromises—it doesn't capitulate. It's tolerant, but not timid.

Prudence asks: "If there is no consensus, how do we form one? What means of reform are available to us? How, lawfully, can we change the law?"

And here is where the difference between power and authority comes in. In the best of worlds, the law commands both. The law confers power on rightful authority, and invests authority with power. The integrity of our laws rests on a continuity, a corpus juris reflecting the accumulated experience of our civilization. Laws are the conventional application of permanent principles. And if democratic government depends on any one central idea, it's that raw power alone, laws that flout those permanent principles, cannot command our respect. Our obedience, yes. Our allegiance, no.

Alexander Hamilton put it this way: "The sacred rights of mankind are not to be rummaged for among old parchments or musty records. They are written, as with a sunbeam, in the whole volume of human nature, by the hand of Divinity itself; and can never be erased or obscured by mortal power." Even the more secular-minded Thomas Jefferson agreed: The "only firm basis" of freedom, he wrote, is "a conviction in the minds of people that their liberties are the gift of God."

American history has had its dark moments, but only twice has this principle been radically betrayed. Only twice has mortal power, using the instrument of the law itself, sought to exclude an entire class of people from their most sacred human rights.

This place in which we meet today marks the first time.

One hundred and thirty-six years ago, a human being was declared a piece of property, literally led off in chains as people of good conscience sat paralyzed by a ruling of the court.

The other time was January 22, 1973. An entire class of human beings was excluded from the protection of the state, their fate declared a "private" matter. That "sunbeam" Hamilton envisioned, the Creator's signature on each new life, was deflected by human hands. No one has ever described what happened more concisely than Justice Byron White in his dissent. It was an act of "raw judicial power" — power stripped of all moral and constitutional authority.

Roe v. *Wade* was not, then, one more natural adaptation in our constitutional evolution. It was not like *Brown* v. *Board of Education*, a refinement extending law and liberty to an excluded class. Just the opposite: It was an abrupt mutation, a defiance of all precedent, a disjuncture of law and authority. Where we used to think of law as above politics, in *Roe* law and politics became indistinguishable. How strange it is to hear abortion now defended in the name of "consensus." *Roe* itself, the product of a contrived and fraudulent test case, was a judicial decree overruling a consensus expressed in the laws of most states. It arose not from the wisdom of the ages or from the voice of the people, but from the ideology of the day and the will of a determined minority. It compels us to ignore the consensus of mankind about the treatment of the unborn. It commands us to disregard the clearest of Commandments. After twenty long years, the people of the United States have refused to heed that command.

Roe v. *Wade* is a law we must observe but never honor. In Hamilton's phrase, it's a piece of "parchment," a musty record bearing raw coercive power and devoid of moral authority. It has done its harm and will do much more. But those who say we must learn to live with it still don't get it. Ultimately, *Roe* cannot survive alongside our enduring, unshakable sense of justice. It is no more permanent than any other act of human arrogance. It is no more unchangeable than the laws which sent Dred Scott back to his master.

This has been the generation of what Malcolm Muggeridge called "the humane holocaust." The loss can never be recovered. Indeed, it can't even be calculated. Not even the familiar statistic—1.6 million a year—begins to express the enormity of it. One person's life touches so many others. How can you measure the void left when so many people aren't even permitted to live among us?

The best we can do is change what can be changed, and, most importantly, stay the course.

And there is no need to wait for some political consensus to form. That consensus is here, and it grows every time someone looks for the first time at a sonogram. It needs only leaders—prudent, patient leaders. It doesn't need apologists to soothe us into inaction. It needs statesmen who will work for change—change here and now.

So, we must ask ourselves, what must the role of the pro-life public official be in 1993 in the face of the catastrophic human carnage of abortion?

Let me be specific.

First, relentless, outspoken opposition to passage of the so-called Freedom of Choice Act.

Second, continuous effort to expand and enlarge the protection of human life in state and national laws and policies.

Third, a continuous drumbeat of public expression which makes the American people confront the facts about abortion in all of its evil.

Fourth, advocacy of a New American Compact in this country which seeks to involve all public and private institutions in a fight for policies and programs to offer women meaningful alternatives to abortion and to offer children and families the help they need to live decent, healthy and happy lives.

Fifth, political action which challenges both major parties and their candidates to protect human life and works for change in national elections.

The need for constancy, activism and relentless effort cannot be overstated. In light of recent events, there is no doubt that this country faces a crisis of awesome dimensions.

National commentators want to treat this issue as settled. We can never let them get away with that. This issue will never die. It will never be "over."

We live in a time of anarchy—when those who claim the right to choose deny pro-life advocates the right to speak. Our voices must be even more determined in response.

In summary, the role of the public official must be to lead—to stand up and say to the people of this country who believe in protecting human life: Press On!

Let this, then, be our clarion call, our call to arms, the keynote of this gathering: Press On!

ROBERT P. CASEY was elected governor of the Commonwealth of Pennsylvania in 1986 and reelected in 1990 in the biggest landslide in Pennsylvania gubernatorial history. In a stunning rejection of the conventional wisdom, he defeated a pro-choice Republican by over one million votes.

A strong fiscal conservative and former Pennsylvania auditor general, Governor Casey consistently ran a tight ship. He brought reform to the state welfare system, cut personal income taxes, invested in law enforcement and drug prevention and treatment, created new jobs, fostered economic development, and cut business taxes. When he left office, Pennsylvania had both the lowest per-capita tax burden of any major Northeastern state, and the lowest number of state employees per capita in the nation.

As the *Philadelphia Daily News* reported at the end of his term: "By nearly any measure, Casey leaves Pennsylvania a better place than it was eight years ago."

In June 1995, Governor Casey founded the Campaign for the American Family, Inc., a lobbying group, and the Fund for the American Family, Inc., a foundation. Both organizations seek to make the well-being of America's families the top priority in formulating social and economic policy in America.

Governor Casey is also an active spokesperson and president of TRIO (Transplant Recipients International Organization), an advocacy group for organ recipients, donor families, and those on the waiting list for organs.

He and his wife, Ellen, live in Scranton. Married for forty-three years, they have eight children and twenty grandchildren.

CAMPAIGN FOR THE AMERICAN FAMILY, INC.
FUND FOR THE AMERICAN FAMILY, INC.
1555 Wilson Boulevard, Suite 300
Arlington, Virginia 22209
703.875.8724   703.522.4969 (fax)   800.420.8733